To Rimjhim
with love and
best wishes –

Amjadalikhan

Regards and love.

[signature]

All good
Wishes

[signature]

Aug 11th, 2004

Abba . . .
God's Greatest Gift to Us

Family Pride

Abba . . .
God's Greatest Gift to Us

Amaan Ali Bangash
Ayaan Ali Bangash

Lustre Press
Roli Books

'The pursuit of perfection, then, is the
pursuit of sweetness and light.'

ISBN: 81-7436-212-6

Text: © Amaan Ali Bangash & Ayaan Ali Bangash 2002
Photographs and documents: © Amjad Ali Khan,Amaan &
Ayaan Ali Bangash private collection

© Roli & Janssen BV 2002
Published in India by
Roli Books in arrangement
with Roli & Janssen BV
M-75 Greater Kailash-II (Market)
New Delhi 110 048, India.
Phone: 6442271, 6462782
Fax: 6467185
Email: roli@vsnl.com
Website: rolibooks.com

Printed and bound at Singapore

Contents

Acknowledgements

We had never in our wildest dreams, thought that we would be writing a book on our father, especially at such an early stage of our lives. It gives us great joy and happiness to share the various stages and moments of the life of a great man whom we call Abba.

We would like to thank first and foremost, Abba for all his time and patience right from day one of this work. Maa, thank you for your support and help for all the facts and details. We would like to thank our dear friend, Amritha Venkatraman for all her help and support. We would also like to thank the photographers whose photographs feature in this book. We have special memories attached to each one of their photographs. Last but not the least, our thanks to all at Roli Books. Thank you for the trust and energy that you invested in us to be able to come out with this.

This book is not a professional analysis of our father but a perception of the human being behind the musician known to the world as Amjad Ali Khan.

Amaan Ali Bangash
Ayaan Ali Bangash

Abba—Our Father and Guru

Romance fails and so do friendships, but the relationship of father and child, less noisy than all others, remains indelible and indestuctible, the strongest relationship on earth.

– Theodor Reik

K nown to the world as Ustad Amjad Ali Khan, we feel euphoric to be the only ones to call this great icon of music, Abba. An exceptional provider, incomparable father, disciplined guru, dedicated husband and an outstanding human being – that's the Abba we know. We feel extremely fortunate to have been born as his sons and believe that our good fortune is the result of some auspicious deed that we must have performed in our past lives. Most of what we are today can be attributed to the superior guidance that our father has provided us with. This guidance has followed the path of traditional values set against the background of an ocean of music. Our first tryst with music came at a very early age – as early as a day old. According to family reminiscences, Abba sang to each of us when we were being brought home from the hospital. Perhaps the guru in him awoke from that very day!

Abba introduced the *sarod* to us as a way of life, not as a subject that would require lessons. Like all other children, our days were divided into lunchtimes, nap times, playtimes, and homework times. However, unlike other children, we had a *sarod* time too! Once we got back from school, lunch was followed by a short nap and homework,

FACING PAGE:

Abba with Amaan and Ayaan, Mumbai 2000.

At a photo shoot by Gautam Rajadhyaksha in between one of our recordings in Mumbai. Abba looked as elegant as ever.

11

TOP:

Abba with Amaan (left) and Ayaan (right).

Thrilling times for us as kids when Abba would play our nursery rhymes on his sarod. This was his master stroke in connecting us with the sarod and music.

RIGHT:

Amaan with the *sarod*, while Ayaan looks on.

This baby sarod was a gift to Amaan from Bishan Das Sharma, owner of Rikhi Ram and Sons in New Delhi. Amaan actually played this sarod, as did Ayaan later.

TOP:

Abba, Amaan, Ayaan in the music room. Maa looks on.

Maa's presence in the music room implied 'dignified behaviour' on our part. Once she left, we were back to our old tricks. However, we could not mess with Abba after a point.

LEFT:

Abba with Amaan (left) and Ayaan (right).

Abba has always known what he wanted us to play at different stages. There has been no compromise ever.

RIGHT:

From Abba's dairy.

From 1984 to 1986, Abba kept a diary, in which he wrote about everything.

BOTTOM:

Abba with disciples, Daud Sadozai and Iqbal Narodh, and Amaan on the tabla, London, 1986.

This was our first trip abroad. We attended Abba's concerts in Germany and London, and saw how positively the West reacted to our tradition. Abba, though a frequent traveller, visited the tourist spots for the first time.

Amaan is learning Tilak kamad, Durga and Malkouns. Ayaan also has good sense of tunefulness. He enjoys singing too. Amaan's voice is also very tuneful which is very essential to learn any instrument specially, Sarod.

Abba on stage with Amaan behind, 1989.

Abba often made us sit on stage behind him, even though we were not participating in the performance. We did, however, learn a lot from Abba's interaction with various kinds of audiences.

Abba on stage with Ayaan, 1983.

Memories of this concert still make us laugh. It was Basant Panchami *(welcoming of spring) and Maa had done the stage decor. Once the concert commenced, Maa went to the balcony to take a look at the beautiful stage, when she suddenly saw Ayaan, walking on and taking a seat next to Abba. Maa came running down and tried to bribe Ayaan with chocolates and cold drinks from the wings. Abba behaved as if he did not know the boy, and everyone was relieved when finally, Ayaan went to Maa.*

Ayaan at the *Sarod* Festival in 1988, New Delhi.

This was Ayaan's solo debut on stage. He played Raga Tilak Kamod. *Maa had sprayed our hair that day so that we looked like* decent *children on stage.*

after which we headed to the music room, where Abba either devoted time individually to each of us or taught us together. As kids we found it cumbersome to play an instrument that was much bigger than us in size! Maa would often jokingly remark that it looked like the *sarod* was playing us rather than we were playing the *sarod*! She would also block her ears saying that the sounds we produced in the music room were more noise than music!

Being young children, the initiation of music into our daily life involved great discipline. Abba made great efforts to develop appealing instructional methods so that, as youngsters, we would accept sound and music as a pleasurable way of life. He would make us sing the popular nursery rhymes *Old MacDonald Had a Farm* and *Yankee Doodle*, while he played the tunes on his *sarod*. The amalgamation of our voices and his playing enabled us to connect with the notes behind the words used in the rhymes. We were thrilled

to make this correlation and it was from some of these associations that our love for music took its roots. These elementary learning techniques that Abba incorporated into the intricate process of comprehending Indian classical music, went a long way in the *sarod* becoming a way of life for us. Abba devoted a great amount of time, effort and love towards making us musicians.

Even while Abba silently wished that we would carry on his musical lineage, he never once authoritatively asserted his desire. So though he began our musical training at a very young age, he never forced us to play the *sarod*. He was equally comfortable with the idea of us following non-musical professions. On the other hand, even as children we were perceptive enough to gauge that if we had chosen non-musical careers, deep down in his heart he would have been greatly saddened. Abba often explained to us that since his father had been a great instrumentalist, Abba, perforce, had to be brilliant if not

Amaan at the *Sarod* festival in1988.

Amaan played Raag Yaman. *There were over forty* sarod *players who participated in the festival. Abba's disciples, Gurudev Singh and Narendra Nath Dhar, are also seated.*

superb, at playing the *sarod*. By telling us this, he was trying to explain that if *we* chose to adopt playing the *sarod* as a profession, then we would be expected to carry forward the torch of ancestral perfection. Abba was a great legend's son for whom the path of life had already been formatted – he had had to shoulder the great responsibility of continuing his family's tradition. For us, however, even though we had been born into a musical family, we made a conscious choice ourselves to adopt music as our profession.

We began to accompany our father to his concerts as toddlers. Around the ages of ten and eight, respectively (Amaan being ten and Ayaan eight), we began to carefully observe Abba giving public recitals. We realized that the receptiveness and acceptance by an audience is a musician's most valued gift. To be able to make the audience smile, laugh, cry or listen silently is the proof of an artiste's genius! As we grew older, there were times when we re-thought our professional decision; however our love for the instrument and the audience kept drawing us back. Of course our devotion to the *sarod* has been so intense primarily because we have had the gift of having the best possible guru as our father. Therefore, it goes without saying that we owe him our profession.

To be our guru and to impart to us the age-old musical legacy of the Senia-Bangash family was a hard task for Abba. The Senia-Bangash School of Music, as it is popularly known, is an interpretation of the Senia School, named after Akbar's famous court musician, Tansen. We were normal kids, constantly playing pranks such as pushing our *sarods* away, putting powder all over our father's students and jumping around the music room. Even though Abba did not approve of these 'misdemeanours', he did not lose his temper, realising that such pranks were a normal part of our growing up. If at all, he tried to curb us gently. That is not to say that he never lost his temper. He most certainly did when he thought we had crossed certain limits. For instance once Abba was teaching Ayaan a *taan* in *Raga Malkauns*. The moment Ayaan learnt the *taan*, he switched over to *Raga Yaman* without Abba's permission, just like that. Furious,

Abba at Mian Tansen's tomb.

Abba feels very fortunate to have been born in Gwalior. This is a very sacred city for musicians as the tomb of the great vocalist Mian Tansen, the immortal musician at Emperor Akbar's court, rests here. Our family belongs to the Senia School, hence this connection makes the ties all the more spiritual.

Abba and Dada Abba.

Haafiz Ali Khan was conferred with an honorary doctorate before the concert by the Khairagarh University, Madhya Pradesh, in 1964.

Abba got up from the practice session and left the room. He later patiently explained to Ayaan that each and every raga was a living entity and if it was not give its due respect, then even the raga could curse the player. He had considered Ayaan's flippant switch to another raga an indirect insult to the *sarod*. The *sarod* was and still continues to be godly for him. He has repeatedly and firmly imparted this message to us. Regarding it as a soulmate, he has always taught us to respectfully touch our forehead on the *sarod* before playing it and take permission from any elders present before commencing – be it at home or in a concert hall. Disrespect to music is the biggest offence in Abba's eyes and he loses his temper when its sanctity is tampered with.

Another moot point is that Abba has never differentiated between us and his other students by singling us out for praise or criticism after a performance. The only advice that he has always given is: after a performance, 'hear the recording [of the concert] and you will know how much and what you have to work on or if you are on the right track'. Today we understand the subtlety of this approach to correction. Not many people can accept criticism in a positive manner. Abba, knowing that as hot-blooded youngsters we were likely to sulk at being criticised, adopted this strategy. This approach had a tremendous impact on our professional and personal development. We began to hear our recordings over and over again, often exclaiming 'Eeks' at them. Abba also encouraged us to hear his recordings and those of our grandfather's contemporaries so we could study their interpretation of each raga and imbibe the best from their work. Listening to a plethora of Indian classical musicians, we have been able to enlarge our canvas with the aid of new ideas and talents. Abba has

taught us to never look down upon any artist; rather to look for his good points. His teaching highlights the constant need to be humble, to follow a humanitarian code of conduct and consistently practise in order to improve our art.

The time we have spent in the music room has enabled the relationship between Abba and us to flourish in two dimensions – as a guru and his *shishyas*, and as a father with his sons. Accompanying Abba to his lecture demonstrations and concerts has provided us with ample opportunities to observe his interaction with a large cross-section of audiences and the state of ecstasy he goes into as he lovingly moves his fingers over the strings of his *sarod*. We have also observed the way he teaches his students.

Even though Abba's father, Ustad Haafiz Ali Khan passed away in 1972, Abba continues to feel his father's presence at all times. Not many would believe this, but Abba feels he continues to receive occasional training from his father in his dreams. By sharing his dreams with us, Abba made us realize that without a guru's blessings and teachings, a disciple was like an illegitimate child. Abba has never forced us to treat him like a guru. He has only asked of us to be good human beings. He believes that if at an early age, a person's character has not taken a humane path, then it will be hard to modify it in the years to come. Therefore tolerance, patience and perseverance should be inculcated right from the start. Further, Abba emphasises that, as musicians, we must never blow our own trumpet, work hard, and believe in destiny as well as in the Almighty. By emphasising such ideologies and beliefs, he has endeavoured to

Dada Abba (centre), with sons, Abba (left) and Rehmat Ali Khan (right).

Nikhil Ghosh plays the tabla and Shubroto Roy Choudhury, the tanpura. *The concert was organized by the Lalit Kala Music Festival, Kolkata, 1961.*

21

clearly demonstrate the age-old *guru-shishya parampara* or tradition, as well as the discipline that goes along with being a virtuoso.

Seldom do performing musicians give such importance to their families at the peak of their careers. However, despite having a very busy schedule, Abba has always seen to it that he has been there for us whenever we needed him, even though it may have entailed postponing some important tours abroad. He once refused a prestigious offer to perform which would have provided him with enormous monitory gain, because he wanted to return home in time for Amaan's first birthday. In 1984, he turned down an offer to have a meeting with the musical superstar Michael Jackson in order to spend time with his loved ones after a three-month concert tour.

However, despite its many benefits, the dual relationship of a father and a guru is an intricate one. We have been and are, at times, still confused as to where to draw the line between the guru and the father. When we were eight and ten years old, respectively, we accompanied our father to musical gatherings where eminent artists from a variety of disciplines were present. At such gatherings it was customary for Abba to rise from his seat to greet a guest, and for Abba's disciples to get up along with their guru as a matter of respect. At such moments, being disciples of Ustad Amjad Ali Khan, we too, were expected to rise along with his other disciples. However, since Ustad Amjad Ali Khan was Abba to us, and we had seen him get up from his seat a million times in the house, we did not think it necessary to rise along with his other disciples. It took us some time to realize that on such occasions, Abba was only our guru!

As we grew older and became *sarod* players ourselves, we realized that a man of his musical stature and genius is born only once in a thousand years. When we heard Abba's *sarod* recordings and compared them with those of *sarod* players of the past, we realized that his music had increased the expressive scope of the instrument – he had literally made the instrument sing! Over the years, we have been witness to his canvas growing larger and more diverse. Today Abba is an institution in himself and for us, the ultimate guru.

Abba in a pensive mood.

This photograph was taken in Kolkata in 1993. Abba is wearing one of his favourite watches that Maa had presented him with on one of his birthdays.

23

The Growing Years

*He who would leap high
must take a long run.*

– Danish proverb

In the 1930s, the godfather of instrumental music, Ustad Haafiz Ali Khan, our Dada Abba, resided in Gwalior, Madhya Pradesh, in a colony called Jivaji Ganj (now known as Haafiz Ali Khan Marg). His marriage to Dilwari Begum produced two children – Mubarak Ali Khan and Phundan Khan. Unfortunately, a few years after their marriage, Dilwari Begum died of ill health. After her death, on his mother's insistence, Dada Abba remarried – a girl from Shah Jehanpur, called Rahat Jehan, our Dadi Ammi. By 1945, Dada Abba and Dadi Ammi had three children who were named Anwar Khan, Rehmat Ali Khan and Sarwar Khan.

On 9 October 1945, in Gwalior, two years before Indian independence, the music world was given a great gift. The gift came in the form of a baby boy born to Dada Abba and Dadi Ammi. Initially named Masoom, a few months later, a fakir suggested to his parents that Amjad would be a more auspicious name for the child. And so it was. Dadi Ammi often said that Amjad's birth was unplanned.

Abba was the youngest of six brothers and sisters and closest to his sister Sarwar. In fact, Sarwar died in 1971, and to save Dada Abba from the emotional shock, the family concealed her death from him for a time. Being the youngest, Abba was pampered to such an extent by almost all the female members of his family that when he sneezed, four people held out a handkerchief for him in no time! However, Dadi Ammi was a strict mother in many ways. On a cold winter morning, if she saw Abba without his warm clothes,

FACING PAGE:

Abba with his pet bird in Gwalior, 1950s.

Abba tells us that once Dada Abba saw a man selling many birds in a cage in Gwalior. He got so upset that he bought all the birds and released them in a park nearby.

she would pinch him hard so that he learnt a lesson and stayed warm.

When Abba was seven, Madhav Umdakar, Karunesh Kumar Dubey and his nephew Rais Khan were his closest friends. Rais in particular used to hero-worship him. This group of young friends was known for its share of pranks. One of their better known ones was placing a coin in the middle of the road with a string attached. If a pedestrian walked past and bent down to pick up the coin, being ignorant about the attached string, the young boys would tug at the string and pull the coin away. This would leave the stranger highly embarrassed, especially when the boys stood around and laughed.

Dada Abba and Dadi Ammi began to discipline Abba at a very young age. Abba's *namaz* lessons began when he was four years old. A priest was assigned to this task. Dada Abba would often go to the mosque next to their house in Jivaji Ganj to give the *azaan* – the call for prayers.

The *sarod* was, of course, put into Abba's lap even before he knew his own name. In accordance with the age-old musical legacy followed by the Bangash family, Dada

26

LEFT:

Six-year-old Abba performing in Gwalior.

A concert in honour of Mr. Ho Chi Minh and the Vietnamese delegation, 1951. The Congress leader, Mr. Prem Chand Kaushyap is seen behind Abba. Sajjan Lal plays the tabla.

MIDDLE:

Abba with neighbours during Holi, New Delhi 1958.

BOTTOM:

Haafiz Ali Khan's regal personality mesmerized people.

Abba assumed the role of Abba's guru. Originally from Central Asia, the Bangash tribe migrated to India in the 1800s and Haafiz Ali Khan, thereafter, followed its legacy. There was a vast age difference between Abba and his father. Hence, the relationship between the two was more of a guru and a disciple. Long practice sessions and musical discussions with Dada Abba formed a strict routine for most of Abba's adolescent years. However Abba's love for the *sarod* emanated from his heart. When Abba practised late at night, Dada Abba would get up from his sleep and ask him to stop. When Dada Abba fell off to sleep, Abba would sit down again to practise until the wee hours of the morning. Along with the *sarod*, Abba received

Dada Abba and Rai Chand Boral, Kolkata, 1940s.

Rai Chand Boral was a famous music director of Bengal, and a great admirer and friend of Dada Abba. On knowing Rai Chand Boral's interest in the tabla, Dada Abba invited the great Masit Khan from Rampur to teach Rai Chand Boral. This became a historic incident as it led to the establishment of the Rampur Farrukabad Gharana in Kolkata too.

lessons in the tabla and in vocal music from local teachers. He always had a great passion for the tabla. On one occasion, Dada Abba hid the tabla because Abba was spending more time on it than the *sarod*! Abba still tries to keep up his interest in the tabla with his *sarod*-playing.

Although Abba was attached to both his parents, his relationship with his father was dominated by the *guru* factor; he was, however, very close to his mother whom he affectionately called Baaji.

The atmosphere in the 300-year-old Bangash household was such that there was music oozing out of every brick. For generations, members of the Bangash household had been deeply involved with music. Our first known ancestor was Mohammad Hashmi Khan Bangash, who was followed by Gulam Bandegi Khan Bangash. The next, Gulam Ali Khan Bangash, modified the *rabab* into the *sarod*. The *sarod* is, therefore, a relatively young instrument as compared to other instruments of ancient India. Gulam Ali Khan had three sons: Asghar Ali Khan, Murad Ali Khan and Nanneh Khan, who was Dada Abba's father. The treasury of musical compositions in our family started with Nanneh Khan, and we continue to play them even now.

In fact, a tree planted by Ustad Nanneh Khan in the courtyard of the house in Gwalior, still stands today.

Since Nanneh Khan died when Dada Abba was young, he learnt his lessons from Ustad Wazir Khan, a direct descendent of Mian Tansen, the great musician of Emperor Akbar's court. Dada Abba's family was enraged since Wazir Khan was not from the Bangash family, but Dada Abba was not deterred.

Over the years, every male member of the Bangash family remained wrapped up in some form of music. This common love went a long way towards encouraging the development of Abba's musical sensitivities. Though Abba's musical training was imbibed from his father, during his growing years, the main inspiration came from his first cousin, Ahemad Ali Khan. They used to practise together often, and Abba spoke highly of his cousin's musical ability. Other members of the Bangash household also enjoyed playing the *sarod*. Rehmat Ali Khan, Abba's older brother, was deeply into understanding and perfecting the art of *sarod*-playing. Yakub Ali Khan, Abba's uncle, was yet another *sarod* wizard. Nabbu Khan, Dada Abba's younger brother, taught the *sarod* to youngsters, while Mubarak Ali Khan, Abba's stepbrother, also loved the *sarod*. All these factors went a long way towards laying the foundation in Abba's development as an *Ustad* or Learned One.

Another tradition of the Bangash family that Abba inherited was a love for eating: the Bangash family was a great connoisseur of the

TOP:

Ustad Wazir Khan, a direct descendant of Mian Tansen.

Dada Abba was the first sarod *player to learn from Ustad Wazir Khan, a* rudra been *player.*

BOTTOM:

Haafiz Ali Khan, his eldest son, Mubarak Ali Khan (right), his nephew, Ahemad Ali Khan (left), Madhav Singh on the *pakhawaj*, with his brother, the guitarist Gopal Singh.

different varieties of Indian cuisine. Dadi Ammi had many relatives
from Rampur in Uttar Pradesh who were kind enough to impart to
her, delicacies from the Rampuri style of cooking. Since Rampuri
cuisine was extremely time consuming, the Bangash family had to
plan the menu for each meal hours in advance. So, during breakfast,
the menu for lunch was decided, and so on . . . . Abba still loves good
food! However he never complains if the food is not up to the
standard. Some of Dadi Ammi's preparations that Abba still talks
about are *Kachhi Tikki, Dal Gosht* and *Palak Gosht.*

Despite their long-term association with Gwalior, in 1957, the
Bangash family decided to move to New Delhi. Dada Abba decided on
this residential move because compared to Gwalior, Delhi was more
'centrally located', and Dada Abba could enhance the scope of his
musical association, and offer a wider range of opportunities to his
children. Upon the family's arrival in the capital, Dada Abba admitted
Abba into Modern School at Barakhamba Road. The lifestyle that the
Bangash family would lead in Delhi was totally dissimilar to what it
had been used to for the past three hundred years in Gwalior. As
compared to the culture and pace of existence in their ancestral city,
life lead by Delhiites seemed totally different and unusually more

TOP:

Abba with a group of
musicians and dancers during
the Holi festival.

*Birju Maharaj is seen right
behind Abba. New Delhi, 1958.*

BOTTOM:

Abba performing in his School
on UN Day, New Delhi, 1961.

Abba performing with
Shamta Prasad at the Modern
School Founder's Day, early
'60s.

*Shamta Prasad was Abba's
regular accompanist during the
'60s. He had a great fondness for
Abba, so much so that he agreed
to play with Abba at this
Founder's Day function of his
school for a nominal amount.*

demanding to the Bangash family at first. In order to feel comfortable in his new home and at ease with the culture of the city, Abba had to make certain changes in his everyday life. The school was more diverse in every which way and offered a tremendous challenge. Abba had to accommodate the increased demands of his new school with the requirement of intense musical training. He tells us that his routine started with practice early in the morning, followed by school till the afternoon, and then practice, more practice and yet more practice! Even during this tedious daily schedule, he was so dedicated to music that he managed to get special permission from the then principal of Modern School, Mr M.N. Kapoor, to skip the games periods to continue with his own practice. Even though they lived close to school and Abba was able to cycle there, the routine did prove to be extremely taxing.

Other adjustments had to be made too. The school was filled with children from business households. For a child to resist peer pressure and have the courage and conviction to pursue a musical career was no mean task. He often had to face taunts and jibes for not partaking in fun activities, but took it in his stride, trying, whenever he could, to spend time with his friends and go out for the usual lunches and movies. He had no qualms about the fact that he had a tough road

ahead to be able to balance school, homework, *sarod* practice and fun. His childhood friends were later to remark that they had never seen anyone so young with such great determination and focus on achieving his goal.

Abba always maintained that he owed a great deal to his teachers who were very supportive of his cause. Due to his humble nature and perseverance, he endeared himself to them. He was asked to play the *sarod* on various occasions, and willingly partook in these functions.

On one such occasion, he amused the audience by playing the famous 1960's song *Come September* on his *sarod*!

As time passed, Abba's musical talent flourished, and word about his outstanding aptitude spread among members of the Indian classical circle. Having the added advantage of being Ustad Haafiz Ali Khan's son, Abba was offered some excellent opportunities to perform at prestigious music festivals. He started at a young age, from 1951 onwards, and soon, his career graph began to ascend steadily. Abba's debut concerts took the audiences by storm. By the early '60s, his exceptional musical capabilities led him to be bracketed with learned musicians twice his age. Amjad Ali Khan's participation became a must for every music festival. He, however, maintains that he was no child prodigy and had to work his way to the top.

Abba, early '60s.

Abba's friends were amazed by his single-minded dedication. The sarod *seen in the photograph was used by Abba extensively during the '60s, and is today displayed in the Museum in Sarod Ghar, Gwalior.*

TOP:

Left to right: Bismillah Khan, Dada Abba, Ghulam Mustafa Khan, Nissar Hussain Khan, unknown, Mushtaq Hussain Khan, Kanthe Maharaj, Ravi Shankar, Ali Akbar Khan, Radhika Mohan Moitra, Vilayat Khan, Kishan Maharaj and Keramatullah Khan.

BOTTOM:

Three legends together.

Haafiz Ali Khan (first row, second from left), Faiyaaz Khan and Ahemad Jaan Thirakhwa.

For various reasons other members of the family who were older than him were unable to make a mark in the music world. Perhaps the Almighty selects certain people for greatness – He certainly chose Abba for the *sarod*. Since Abba became an *Ustad* at the age of fifteen itself, he had to interact with people much older than himself. Even his accompanists were twice his age. However, despite this age barrier, they always respectfully addressed him as Khan Saheb, thus demonstrating reverence not only to Abba, but also to his musical lineage. In the 1960s, the Modern School Principle, Mr M.N.Kapoor, asked Abba to play for the school's Founders Day. Abba accepted this invitation and humbly requested the renowned tabla player, Pandit Shamta Prasad to accompany him. Since Pandit Shamta Prasad was genuinely fond of Abba, he gladly agreed and accepted the nominal contribution the school had to offer.

Dada Abba was very proud of his son's achievements though he never mentioned them. He was especially proud that Abba had made a mark for himself in the world of music without the patronage of any institute, senior musician or, for that matter, any godfather. It was the appreciation that he got from his listeners that made him an

A reception for Dada Abba at Rabindra Sadan, Kolkata, 1967.

Abba, Radhika Mohan Moitra and Birendra Kishore Roy Choudhury are also seen. This was one of Dada Abba's last trips to Kolkata, a city that adored him no end. He was felicitated in Kolkata that evening and the ceremony was followed by Abba's recital of Raga Mian Ki Malhar. *He was accompanied by Shamta Prasad.*

Ustad when he was still in his shorts! Abba was first lovingly called *Ustad* by the organisers of the Sadarang Music Festival held in Kolkata in 1958. At that time he was all of twelve years of age, and played *Raga Gujri Todi,* accompanied by Ustad Keramat Khan on the tabla.

Abba recalls an amusing incident that occurred in Allahabad in 1959. His name was printed as *Ustad* Amjad Ali Khan in the publicity brochure athough he was still in his teens! On arriving at the Allahabad railway station, there was no one there to receive him. After hours of waiting, a man of the Prayag Sangeet Samiti very hesitantly approached him and asked if *he* was indeed Ustad Amjad Ali Khan. When Abba cleared his doubt, the man told Abba that he had been expecting a huge man with a turban and a beard and not a young boy!

The '60s played a major role in Abba's life. Dada Abba's health had deteriorated and he was not performing frequently. Consequently, instrumentalists from other schools of music began to dominate the scene. The ugly face of rivalry and power politics emerged, resulting in these other musicians becoming hostile towards Haafiz Ali Khan Saheb and his young and upcoming son. This did not, however, deter Abba, who pursued his craft, while steering clear of controversy. Believing God to be his only earnest friend, he continued to enhance his skills.

Since Abba's composing was still in a nascent stage, he needed to allow established musical approaches to influence his art. Thus, he sought and absorbed every note and nuance he could from the music of the most prominent musical legends of the 1950s. Even when one hears Abba playing today, flashes of the individual styles of these greats reflect in his playing. His *Raga Pilu* seems to replicate the vocal chords of Ustad Abdul Karim Khan; his *Marwa* is a reminder of Amir Khan's voice, and, of course, the magic of Kesar Bai Kerkar resonates prominently in his music. Other performers that Abba associated with closely during the '50s were Pandit Shambu Maharaj, Ustad Bade Gulam Ali Khan, Ustad Ahemad Jaan Thirakhwa, Ustad Waheed Khan, Pandit Omkar Nath Thakur and Pandit Kanthe Maharaj. He cherishes fond memories of them.

There is one person in Abba's life whose relationship with him cannot be described in words. To call him Abba's friend is an understatement. This special friend is Arup Kumar Sarkar, whom we call Arup Chacha. Abba and Arup Chacha met in 1964, and ever since, their friendship has grown stronger with each passing year, with Chacha being a constant source of inspiration, motivation and strength. Abba says: 'He is a greater son of Haafiz Ali Khan than I.' Their mutual respect and love permeates through both our families.

Even though Abba achieved many professional accolades during his young days, his personal life was not devoid of struggle. On the home front, he was confronted with enormous pressures and

FACING PAGE:

Abba, 1967.

He continued to make a mark without the patronage of any institute throughout the decade. Abba's journey has been a private one.

Dada Abba.

We really wish that we could have physically seen Dada Abba. He was one of the greatest instrumentalists of the last century. We are so fortunate to be featured in an album called Legendary Lineage *that contains the music of Dada Abba, Abba and both of us. Since Dada Abba was against recordings, these pieces of his music were his live performances compiled together and released in 1997.*

commitments. He had to look after his family since Dada Abba was growing old. And since Abba was one of the primary earning members in his family, the responsibility of getting his sisters married fell on him. Abba often narrates the story of his sister Sarwar's marriage to us as an example of the emotional and financial hardships he faced when he was in his early twenties. It so happened that that after taking on the financial responsibility of his sister's wedding, he went to check his bank balance, to discover that he had only ninety-six rupees in his account! This naturally gave him a jolt. However, he decided not to worry Dada Abba by telling him about the pittance he had. Instead, he decided to work hard, play at more concerts and gradually re-build the bank balance by himself. Apart from this, Abba's family also used to send allowances to other family members living in Gwalior. Bowed down under such extensive financial responsibilities, Abba went to work silently in order to fulfil his domestic obligations. His life was certainly not a piece of cake! In fact, Abba maintains that he grew up faster than most of his peers because he was constantly interacting with people twice his age and combating problems that are usually handled by older members of a family.

One of our favourite stories of Abba's struggling years is when he was pick-pocketed on a railway station while on his way home. His concert fee was pick-pocketed at Kolkata railway station, so he borrowed money from the porter and gave it to the taxi driver. He paid the porter by borrowing from his fellow passenger in the train. Once he reached Delhi, he borrowed money from the porter on the Delhi station to repay his travelling companion. It did not end there! He borrowed money from the taxi driver in Delhi to pay the porter, and finally paid the taxi driver when he reached home! Abba's domestic struggles were annunciated when in 1972, Dada Abba fell seriously ill and lay dying from various old-age problems. However, even on his deathbed, Dada Abba expressed gratitude to God for the blessings that he had showered upon his son. During this time, Dada Abba told his disciple and noted *sursingar* (ancient stringed instrument invented

LEFT:

Dada Abba's *mazaar* in New Delhi.

Dada Abba's mazaar *rests in New Delhi next to Hazrat Nizamuddin Auliya's* dargah. *It was Dada Abba's desire to be buried amidst such sacred surroundings.*

BOTTOM:

Abba.

Abba returned to New Delhi from Chennai in time to take part in Dada Abba's last rites.

by Hazrat Amir Khusro) player Birendra Kishore Roy Chowdhury, 'I am old now. Amjad is my clear photograph'. Thus, Dada Abba knew that after him, Abba would be an excellent caretaker of the Bangash household. More importantly, he was certain that he was leaving the institution of the *sarod* in the safest hands possible.

Dada Abba expired in New Delhi on 28 December 1972. On that day, Abba was performing in a concert in Chennai. On hearing the news that his beloved father had died, Abba rushed back. Even though Dada Abba had been bedridden for the past few years, and Abba was aware that he was dying slowly, his actual death was a big blow. As Dada Abba had desired, his grave rested near Hazrat Nizamuddin Auliya's *dargah* in New Delhi.

Attempting to fill the void created in his life by Dada Abba's death, Abba decided to immerse himself in his work and strengthen his relationship with the *sarod*. He kept his morale up by having faith in the Almighty, remembering the *taleem* (upbringing) he had received from his father, drawing from the love he got from his family members, and absorbing the affection of his audience.

Sarod Ghar today.

The ancestral house that has been converted into a museum, one of a kind. It houses all the instruments of some of the great names in the history of Indian classical music. Nanneh Khan, Abba's grand father, planted the beautiful tree in the courtyard.

The Making of
a Maestro

Yesterday is not ours to recover,
but tomorrow is ours to win or lose.

– Lyndon Baines Johnson

With Dada Abba's death, Abba lost his staunchest supporter, mentor, closest companion and spiritual guide. Now he was literally by himself – all alone. It was impossible for him to push the golden years he had spent with Dada Abba to the back of his mind. Even though he performed all his duties diligently, he constantly kept thinking about the times when he had attended and performed in concerts with Dada Abba. Recalling an incident of how, inspired by a noted senior musician, he had got his hair stylishly curled, and how Dada Abba had scolded him, Abba silently wished that his father was there to scold him again.

Abba also recalled how Dada Abba had been against the concept of recording his music on albums. He had looked upon it as a discourtesy to his music. Abba's first album was, however, recorded by Hindustan Records when he was eighteen years old. Listening to a music lover extolling the album, Dada Abba remarked that even though he believed that recording music was ideologically incorrect, Abba must keep up with the times and do what his heart pleased. When Dada Abba died, it dawned upon Abba that his father had loved him so much that he was willing to give up his age-old principles to make his son happy. Abba also remembered how happy Dada Abba had been when he was able to make him travel for the first

FACING PAGE:

Abba tunes his *sarod.*

Abba on stage transforms into a different person – he seems to be connected somewhere else, in a place unseen by us and the people around him.

BOTTOM:

Abba in Mumbai.

He had curled his hair, being inspired by a senior musician. Dada Abba apparently got very upset with Abba about this.

time in an air-conditioned first class train compartment. Abba remembers the joy on his father's face when he took him in his newly acquired car for a medical check-up. Since Abba was and still remains very attached to his father, he believes that even after his death, Dada Abba has continued to live on spiritually in each of his children.

Another point that Dada Abba had insisted on was that after his death, no festivals should be held in his honour. He felt strongly that musicians who partook in such festivals might choose to perform free of cost as a sign of respect, and thus, might lose out on well-deserved earnings. His instructions, therefore, aimed at protecting the interests of his fellow musicians. However, after his father died, Abba and Arup Chacha decided that they would organize music festivals in memory of Dada Abba, but would ensure that musicians were duly paid for their participation. The essence of these music festivals would be to honour Ustad Haafiz Ali Khan and to keep the memory of Dada Abba alive forever. On Dada Abba's first death anniversary (28 December 1973), Abba and Arup Chacha organized the longest every music festival in the history of Indian classical music. Held in Kolkata at Kalamandir, the Haafiz Ali Khan Memorial Music Festival spread over seventeen days. Most eminent Indian classical musicians of the time partook in the festival and paid homage to Dada Abba in their own ways. The true goal of this Festival was to pay a musical tribute to Dada Abba, and provide a revered forum for young, upcoming artists. Abba performed first, playing one of Dada Abba's favourite ragas – *Malkauns*. Many such festivals were organized by Abba in the years ahead.

Abba and Arup Kumar Sarkar, Shantiniketan, 1966.

The beginning of a lifelong friendship, which is not easy to explain. Perhaps even they can't put into words what they really mean to each other.

However, six years later, he decided to discontinue this practice, realizing that musicians were participating in the festivals purely for financial gain, and were perhaps forgetting the symbolic meaning behind them. Once Abba decided to discontinue the Haafiz Ali Khan Music Festivals, he decided to create other means whereby Dada

Abba's memory could be preserved. In 1985, he introduced the Haafiz Ali Khan Awards. These awards are given to musicians who have made an immense contribution in the world of music and have become legends in their own realms. Abba thus became the first musician to honour his fellow musicians. The first two recipients of the Haafiz Ali Khan Awards were Pandit Kishan Maharaj and Pandit Shamta Prashad. In the years that followed the great guitarists John Williams and Julian Bream from the United Kingdom, the world-famous violinists Anne Sophie Mutter of Germany and Igor Frolov of Russia, the Indian classical vocalists Pandit Bhim Sen Joshi and Srimati Girija Devi were among the many gifted artists that were presented with the Haafiz Ali Khan awards. In order to further

Abba at the first Haafiz Ali Khan Music Festival, Kolkata, 1973.

Abba inaugurated the festival by playing Raga Malkauns. *Latif Ahemad played the tabla and Abba's disciples, Gurudev Singh and Asit Ghatak, the* tanpura.

45

Abba presenting the first
Haafiz Ali Khan Award to
Shamta Prasad in Kolkata,
1985.

*Abba is one of the first artistes
to honour and felicitate a fellow
musician. Started in 1985, the
award ceremony takes place
every year and honours artistes
from the world of classical
music, both Indian and Western.*

FACING PAGE:

Abba, Amir Khan and Arup
Kumar Sarkar (in the middle)
at the Haafiz Ali Khan Music
Festival, 1973. Ashit Ghatak
(second from left), an old
disciple and Shyamal Bose
(extreme right), the tabla
player, can also be seen.

*Abba has great regard for Amir
Khan. Once his flight got delayed
before a nightlong music
conference and he arrived after
Amir Khan was already on
stage. According to custom, a
younger artiste could not go and
sit on the stage after a senior
artiste. But on learning of
Abba's late arrival, Amir Khan
forced Abba to sit and play after
him. In fact, he sat in the
audience listening to him after
his own concert!*

TOP:

Abba with Duke Ellington, 1963.

Duke Ellington listens to Abba along with Harry Carney. This picture first appeared in his book, Music Is My Mistress.

RIGHT:

Abba with Heman Chandra Sen, the oldest *sarod* maker in Kolkata.

Hemen Chandra Sen has made Abba's sarods from the '70s. He was honoured in 2002 with the Haafiz Ali Khan Award for his unique contribution. Abba's earlier sarod makers were Gopal & Sons and Govardhan. The latter also made Dada Abba's sarods.

१९७२ में राज्यपाल द्वारा। डाक्ट्रेट फेलोशिप एवं
सन् १९७२ में ही राष्ट्रपति द्वारा 'पद्म श्री' प्राप्त
हुआ। २५ मार्च सन् १९८० में शिक्षा मन्त्री द्वारा
संगीत नाटक अकादमी पुरस्कार प्राप्त।

Pt. Samata Prasad
(GUDAIE MAHARAJ)
C 23/22, Kabir Choura, Varanasi.
C. 25 A-E Ram Katora Road, Varanasi

फोन : ६५१४५
पं0 सामता प्रसाद
(गुदई महाराज)
सी० २३/२२, कबीर चौरा, वाराणसी
सी० २५ ए ई राम कटोरा रोड, वाराणसी
दिनांक ३०.१२.८५

माननीय श्री उस्ताद अमजद अली जी को
नमस्कार,

खुदा आपको सलामत रखें, मुझ गरीब कलाकार का यही
दुआ है 24 Dec.85 को जो आपने मुझे प्रतिष्ठा दिखलाया
है, उसके लिए मैं जीवन-भर आपका एहसानमंद रहूँगा।
खुदा की ओर से आपके लिए और यह दुआ है कि
आपका झंडा विश्व में गड़ेगा। दोनों बच्चों एवं बहू को
दुआ। खत लिखने में कोई भी गल्ती हो तो आप
उसे माफ कीजिएगा।

आपका शुभचिंतक

सामताप्रसाद

पद्मश्री पंडित सामता प्रसाद
सी.२५ए-ई रामकटोरा रोड वाराणसी
सी०२३।२२, कबीरचौरा-वाराणसी

Letter of appreciation (30.12.85) from Pt. Samata Prasad to Abba.

30.12.85

वाराणसी

किशन महाराज

प्रिय अमजद,

सस्नेह दुआ।

तुम्हारा भेजा हुआ पत्र मिला। यह जानकर अत्यन्त प्रसन्नता हुई कि संगीतज्ञों का गौरव बढ़ाने के लिए तुम्हारी संस्था ने उस्ताद हाफीज अली खाँ पुरस्कार हर वर्ष किसी दो कलाकारों को देने का निश्चय किया है और हमारा यह सौभाग्य है कि इस महान विद्वान के पुरस्कार से सर्वप्रथम मैं सम्मानित होने जा रहा हूँ।

मुझे यह सम्मान सहर्ष स्वीकार है।

शेष कुशल।

सद्भावनाओं सहित :—

(किशन महाराज)

सी० २४/६ ए०, कबीर चौरा, वाराणसी (दूरभाष : ६२६७६)

Letter of appreciation (30.12.85) from Kishan Maharaj for receiving the Haafiz Ali Khan award.

TOP:

Pune, 1990 – Abba, Bhimsen
Joshi, Balamurli Krishna.

RIGHT:

Abba and Guitarist John
Williams in London, 1989.

FACING PAGE, TOP:

Abba honours Nusrat Fateh
Ali Khan in Gwalior, 1997.

FACING PAGE, BOTTOM:

Abba and Russian Violinist
Maestro Igor Frolov, Moscow
1987.

*They played a series of concerts
in Russia and India in 1987 and
1988.*

cultural ties between India and Pakistan, Abba extended the Haafiz Ali Khan awards to honourable members of the Pakistani music community as well. Among the Pakistani recipients of the Haafiz Ali Khan awards are vocalists Ustad Nusrat Fateh Ali Khan and Ustad Salamat Ali Khan.

After Dada Abba's death, Abba discovered that he had to do twice as much as he had done when his father was living to keep his family legacy alive. He realized that in order to continue the musical pre-eminence that Dada Abba had displayed, his own musical talents must be enhanced further. He felt that the audience was viewing him now as an individual who no longer had the physical support of his famous father. Thus, the responsibility of performing to the highest levels of excellence fell heavily upon his shoulders.

Family Tree

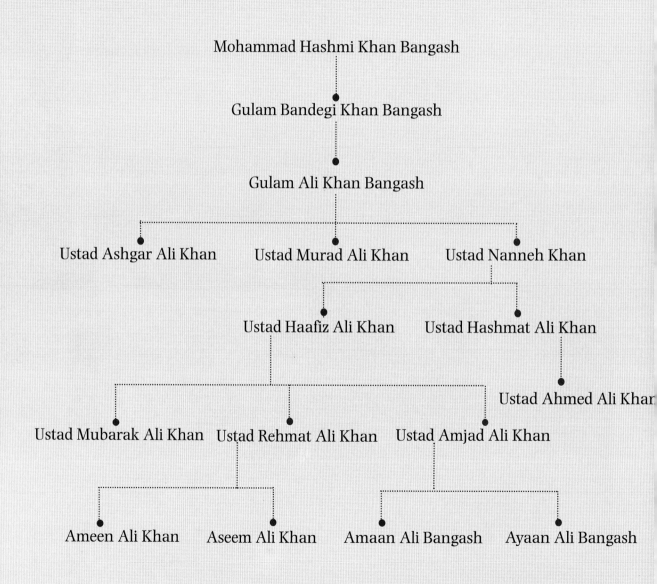

Mohammad Hashmi Khan Bangash

Gulam Bandegi Khan Bangash

Gulam Ali Khan Bangash

Ustad Ashgar Ali Khan   Ustad Murad Ali Khan   Ustad Nanneh Khan

Ustad Haafiz Ali Khan   Ustad Hashmat Ali Khan

Ustad Ahmed Ali Khan

Ustad Mubarak Ali Khan   Ustad Rehmat Ali Khan   Ustad Amjad Ali Khan

Ameen Ali Khan   Aseem Ali Khan   Amaan Ali Bangash   Ayaan Ali Bangash

MOHAMMAD HASHMI KHAN BANGASH

GULAM BANDEGI KHAN BANGASH

GULAM ALI KHAN BANGASH

USTAD NANNEH KHAN

USTAD HAAFIZ ALI KHAN

USTAD AMJAD ALI KHAN

AMAAN ALI BANGASH

AYAAN ALI BANGASH

A Family Man

*The happiest moments of my life have been
the few which I have passed at home
in the bosom of my family.*

– Thomas Jefferson

Abba was torn between two important aspects of his life; one, the musical legacy that he was to carry forward, and the other, the voice of his heart. Famous for his boyish and well-sculpted looks, his handsome appearance attracted the opposite sex easily. On the other hand, realizing the importance of his musical legacy, he knew he had to be extremely cautious while selecting his life partner. However, this realization did not come till later. Love knows no boundaries and when Abba was twenty-one, he met a beautiful young lady who was older than him by almost ten years. Their love affair lasted for over eight years. Abba was keen to settle early in life, but destiny willed otherwise. In due course, he realized that the lady he loved was not serious about getting married, and Abba felt that he was being used. The relationship gradually tapered off. Hard hit, Abba decided to concentrate more on his music, which he knew would never betray him. Things were not that easy however, and there was unpleasantness since she did not wish to break off the relationship.

Seeing the tension her son was going through, Dadi Ammi pressurized him to get married. In March 1973, she selected a Muslim girl, who was distantly related, and Abba had no choice but to agree. Soon after the wedding, Abba was dismayed to see that he could not relate to his partner, mentally, emotionally and above all, musically. He did try his best to adjust and make his marriage work.

FACING PAGE:

Family picture.

This photo was taken in Maa's family house in Sibsagar, in Assam. Both of us are wearing t-shirts that Abba got for us from one of his tours abroad.

57

Maa at various concerts.

Maa at various concerts.

Maa was undoubtedly one of the most upcoming and sought after danseurs of the early '70s. Even today, we meet people all over the world who say that her leaving dance was a big loss to the world of Bharatnatyam. Other than Rukmini Devi Arundale, one of Maa's teachers who is family to us is Pushpa Shankar.

A beautiful baby girl was born out of this relationship. But matters did not improve and the entire episode ended within a year. In spite of his marriage ending in a fiasco, Abba saw to it that, in due course, his wife remarried according to her own choice of husband, who was also her childhood love.

Abba opted to keep his daughter in his family, so that his ex-wife could start life on a clean state again. He was well aware that being a single parent, he would not be able to do justice to her upbringing. Understanding his emotional agony, his older brother (Taaya Abba), who had no children of his own at that point of time, offered to adopt the child. After much thought and discussion with Dadi Ammi, Abba handed over the baby girl to his brother, once again, leaving his life and destiny in the hands of the Almighty.

However, love was soon to literally come *dancing* into his life. In 1974, Abba was performing at the Kala Sangam Music Festival in Kolkata. After his performance, a stunning young lady was escorted backstage by the organizers of the Festival. She was introduced to Abba as Subhalakshmi Borooah, a Bharatnatyam danseuse who had given a brilliant performance at the first Kala Sangam Festival exactly a year ago. After this brief encounter, later that year Abba happened to be in Kolkata again when Maa was giving a dance performance. Once she took centre-stage, Abba was left spellbound by her beauty, grace and fantastic execution of the ancient dance form. From that moment on, 'he started following her!' He began to make enquiries about Maa's background, and got to know that she

58

was born in Assam on 22 July 1945, and had schooled in Assam and
Delhi. She had trained in Bharatnatyam at Kalakshetra in Chennai
under Rukmini Devi Arundale.

From that performance onwards, Abba tried to attend most of
Maa's concerts whenever possible. In turn, he invited her to his
concerts, especially in Kolkata. Maa's initial admiration for Abba
merely extended to that of a fellow artiste, and she was truly
impressed by his sense of aesthetics and incredible sense of
musical proportion. She also found him charming and, over
the next year, they met often, mostly in Kolkata. Till then, at
least for Maa, marriage was nowhere in the picture.

Abba discovered that music played an important
role in the entire Borooah household. Maa's father was
Shri Parashuram Borooah, a tea industrialist, who had
played the lead role in the first ever Assamese motion
picture called *Joymati*. Her mother was Shrimati
Khiroda Kumari Borooah, and her grandfather, Shri
Lakshmi Ram Borooah was an exponent of Indian

59

Abba and Maa's marriage ceremony.

Maa's uncle, Mr P.C. Borooah, Arup Kumar Sarkar and Mr Ravi Mehta witnessed Maa and Abba's registration. There was a very big reception in Kolkata after the marriage. Kolkata was and still has very emotional memories for our parents.

classical music. Her uncle Shri P.C. Borooah was a former member of the Indian parliament and was the first Assamese gramophone artist to obtain acclaim. Maa's dance training too, had begun at a very early age. In her early years, Maa was trained in the Manipuri style of dance by Guru Rash Bihari Sharma. As a young dancer, her single-minded devotion to the art was overwhelming. Between the ages of eight and twelve she gave Manipuri dance performances in New Delhi, Jaipur, Lucknow and Assam. While pursuing her dancing career during these years, she simultaneously attended school, studying in the Sibsagar High School in Assam, Saint John's Dysation in Kolkata and Queen Mary's School in New Delhi. (In fact, it was a matter of coincidence that Maa sang at the Golden Jubilee celebrations of Queen Mary's School and twenty-five years later, Abba performed at its Diamond Jubilee.) After passing her tenth class examinations, Maa joined the famous dance institution called

Kalakshetra in Chennai and spent fifteen years there. She graduated from Kalakshetra with a first-class diploma in Bharatnatyam, and completed her post-graduation from Kalakshetra itself, passing with distinctions. As she began giving public performances, Maa's style revealed superb training, technical perfection, intrinsic clarity of footwork and maturity beyond her years – as stated by the eminent dance critics of the time, Ranga Rao and Subbudu. Maa was also the blue-eyed disciple of Smt. Rukmini Devi Arundale.

As Abba learnt more about Maa and as he persistently attended her concerts, his romantic feelings for her grew stronger. Maa still did not, however, reciprocate his feelings. One day, acting upon his instincts, Abba made a bold decision to ask for Maa's hand in marriage. He had no way of knowing that Maa was perhaps not ready for marriage at that stage in her life. Although Maa had toured all over the world with the *Kalakshetra* group and was one of the few

Maa and Abba's marriage ceremony.

Abba always respected the rituals of Maa's family. He is seen here putting sindoor on Maa's head.

FOLLOWING PAGES 62-63:

A musical partnership – Leeds, UK, 1978.

After Abba's photo shoot, Maa just sat beside Abba at the request of the photographer and was immediately lost in his music. Abba is seen playing his sarod Ganga here.

dancers who was frequently invited by most well-known organizations of India to perform at various prestigious festivals, performing was just a hobby for her, and she did it just for the love of the art form. It was not a source of professional income.

When Abba proposed to her, she told him that she needed six months to think about it and make her decision. During that six-month period, Abba called Maa's house at vague hours late at night (between his practice hours) to enquire about her decision. On receiving these calls, Maa often wondered if Abba was sane! It was not easy for her to take such an important decision as both of them came from very different backgrounds and it would be an inter-caste marriage. More importantly, Abba was a performing artiste, and led a life that entailed constant travelling. Maa's family was concerned about the instability that could arise in the marriage as a result of both their professional lives. In the meantime, Arup Chacha decided to play Cupid between Maa and Abba. He would have lengthy conversations with Maa, convincing her of Abba's capabilities. After the conversations, he would duly report the outcome of his conversations with Maa to Abba. During the six-month period, after close and personal observations, Maa carefully analyzed Abba's personality and finally agreed to marry him in spite of her family's apprehensions. A straightforward and bold person, Maa's decisions are always made to stay.

Fortunately her family stood by her. When we actually think back on our parents' relationship, it is difficult for us to digest how they eventually got married since they hardly ever met during their courtship! What Maa admired about Abba, and probably, this influenced her strongly in her decision to marry him, was that he told her about his past openly.

Having decided that she was going to marry Abba, during one of her trips to Delhi before her marriage, Maa visited Dadi Ammi. At the time, Abba was away for a concert, but had assigned one of his disciples to act as interpreter to bridge the linguistic gap, because Dadi Ammi conversed in Urdu, and Maa spoke Hindi sporadically, along with Tamil, English and Bengali. As the conversation between Dadi Ammi and Maa began, they discovered a strange coincidence. Dadi Ammi mentioned to Maa that when Abba was born, he had been initially named Masoom. His name had later been changed to Amjad. Maa told Dadi Ammi that her name too had been changed. Her parents had initially called her Rajyalakshmi, but a few months later, after seeing the great Carnatak singer, M.S. Subbulakshmi's film, *Meera*, they had changed Maa's name to Subhalakshmi. At this coincidence, a rapport was established between them instantly. Dadi Ammi began to see a daughter in Maa!

The fact that Maa was a Hindu and Abba was a Muslim never had any significant implication in our parents' lives. Abba never once asked Maa to convert to or adopt Islam. He has always been convinced that when the journey of life ends, all people eventually reach the same destination. Maa and Abba believe in one common religion – one of love, music and humanity. Abba often says, 'Every religion needs music and flowers, but flowers and music do not need a religion.' With these beliefs, Maa and Abba's love blossomed over the years.

Their wedding took place in Kolkata, the city associated with their love, on 25 September 1976. A registered marriage witnessed by close friends and family, the simple ceremony was followed by an

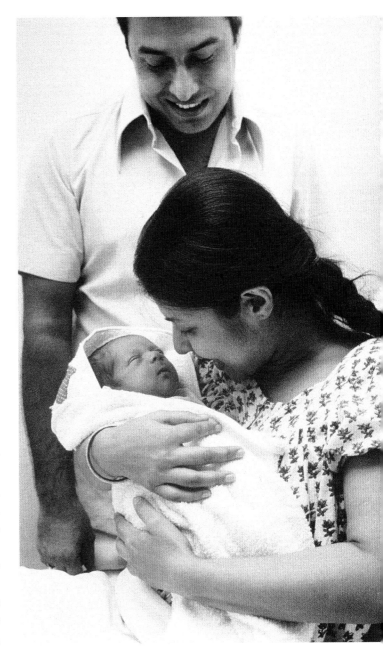

Abba with Amaan (left) and Ayaan (right).

Abba would tell us that a bird would come out of the camera once the photo had been taken, and we would keep waiting for that to happen!

elaborate reception in Kolkata itself that was attended by lots of friends, relatives and various artistes.

After their marriage Maa and Abba spend some time in Ahmedabad and Mumbai. When they were in Mumbai, Maa attended the on-going Haafiz Ali Khan Memorial Festival of 1976. In November of the same year, they left for Hong Kong where Abba was scheduled to perform at the Hong Kong Festival. This was the first time Maa played the *tanpura* with Abba. Thereafter she became his *special tanpura player* on occasions. We remember a time in 1993, when both of us were accompanying Abba, and Maa was playing the *tanpura*. This was the first time all four of us came on stage together. Many such occasions have arisen after that of course.

There is no doubt that Maa did have to make a lot of adjustments in her life after marriage. The first was one that every newly married

Maa and Abba.

Maa has always been a pillar of strength for Abba and a great source of inspiration.

FOLLOWING PAGE 68

TOP:

Drawing by Abba.

We had never seen Abba draw anything ever. Once Ayaan asked him to sketch something in his sketchbook and this is what Abba made.

BOTTOM:

Maa and Abba at Maracas beach in Trinidad, 1992.

We toured the West Indies in 1992, and took a brief holiday too. We drove down from Trinidad to the Maracas beach for a day.

woman makes – sharing her life with her husband. Secondly, as a result of his concert commitments, Abba had to travel constantly, and Maa had to hold fort at home, ensuring that Dadi Ammi's life was comfortable in the absence of her son. As a result of the time they spent together, Dadi Ammi and Maa became very close. Another fact that Maa had to accept and get used to was to incorporate her husband's obligations as a public figure into their life. Being the wife of a person who was constantly in the public eye, she had to be more conscious about her social appearance and activities. Of course, Abba's constant support was a pillar of strength for Maa.

Abba always maintains that Maa has been a precious gift from God to him. Before his marriage, he used to dream of starting a family with a woman who had a compassionate personality. His wishes became a reality. Not only did Maa introduce an atmosphere of domestic discipline into Abba's life, she also created an ambience wherein Abba's artistic and creative talents could flourish freely. She understood him, not only as a musician but also as a person. Her straightforward ways, her love and large heart brought Abba's family happiness and kept them united. Our beloved half-sister, to whom we are extremely close, was very attached to Maa, though she was brought up by our aunt and uncle. Today she is a happily married lady with a wonderful husband and charming daughter.

During the late '60s and early '70s, while Abba experienced

emotional ups and downs, he went through a phase that he still refers to as a 'bad dream'. He had started drinking very heavily, and actually waited for the sun to set so that he could begin his 'session'. He did, however, ensure that he never drank before a concert. Somewhere at the back of his mind he knew that the lifestyle he was following was not very healthy or dignified. Maa's contribution towards bringing his life back to a normal keel cannot be underestimated.

The newly married couple did give a few joint recitals in India and abroad. At these concerts, Maa would give a Bharatnatyam performance in the first half and Abba would take over with a *sarod* recital after the intermission. A year into their marriage, Abba and Maa both decided that they wanted to start a family. Abba was conscious of the fact that as a result of the vast age difference between him and his father, he had not been able to witness Dada Abba's peak as a performing artist, and had only spent a few years with him as a son. Hence he was keen that his children should be able to get the best from him, and spend many years with him.

On 12 July 1977, at Sharma's Nursing Home in New Delhi, a baby boy was born. Named Amaan, which means In the Shelter of God, on the very first day itself, as per the Bangash family tradition, Abba sang a melodious raga into the baby's ear – presumably *Raga Malkauns*. Impatient and excited about sharing his musical legacy with

RIGHT:

Abba and us, at Baden-Baden, 1986.

This was our first visit abroad. Our sarods, *however, travelled with us everywhere, our training proceeding even during this trip.*

BELOW:

Abba and Ayaan going to school.

Abba would often drop us and pick us up from school. He made us learn compositions on the way, and would get very upset at times when we were inattentive. The moment we walked into school, it was like a different world altogether.

his child, Abba presented Amaan with a *baby sarod* a year after his birth. Two years later, another baby boy was born on a sunny afternoon on 5 September 1979. He was named Ayaan – meaning A Gift of God in Turkish, and Eyes in Persian. Once again Abba softly whispered melodious tunes into the newborn's ear (this time, probably *Raga Darbari*). A year later, Abba gave Ayaan the same *baby sarod* that he had given Amaan earlier.

After Ayaan's birth Maa gave up performing. When we grew a little older and started attending school, Maa indirectly received some negative feedback that Abba had suppressed her art, and was not allowing her to perform due to his orthodox thoughts and principles. Saddened by such baseless remarks, Maa took a bold step in keeping with her character. She performed in a farewell concert in New Delhi in 1985 at an overcrowded Siri Fort Auditorium. Maa took centre-stage in the first half, and Abba performed a duet with the noted violinist Lalgudi G. Jayaraman after intermission. The proceeds of the concert went towards a fund collection for an eye hospital. The same year, at the request of Maa's guru, Rukmini Devi Arundale, Maa did a *padam* at the Kalakshetra Festival and bid a final adieu to dance.

70

These two performances were Maa's way of clearing any false impressions about Abba.

Both Maa and Abba welcomed parenthood with open arms. In retrospect, Maa often says that Abba has been an excellent family man – an outstanding father and dedicated husband. Even though Abba was constantly travelling during our growing years, we can never say that he was not there when we needed him. As we grew older and began to attend Modern School in Vasant Vihar, New Delhi, Abba made it a point to drop and pick us up to and from school when he was in town. And, much to our embarrassment, he would occasionally even walk into our classrooms, and all our friends would run to get his autograph. It was so awkward! Once he even prepared our lunch boxes for us. What happened was that Maa developed a fever; the cook was ill, and it was too early for any other staff to report for work. Abba therefore decided to pack our lunch boxes. When lunch hour arrived, we opened our lunch boxes and lo and behold! there were two sandwiches in each box, consisting of plain bread with *aam papad* (sweet and sour) mango candy) in between. We certainly had to struggle hard to bite the bread as it had become hard by then!

Abba explaining a composition to Amaan, London 1996.

Surroundings matter little for Abba when he is teaching something, and he teaches whenever something comes to his mind. Ayaan managed to capture one such moment while waiting for Maa to come out from a store.

Maa playing the *tanpura* for Abba.

Maa is our family's special tanpura *player. She has played the instrument to accompany Abba, mostly abroad and just once or twice in India. There have been times when all four of us have been on stage together.*

It is difficult to remember a time during all these years when we have ever been faced with a NO from Abba. Even before we can voice our needs, our requirements are fulfilled. Abba has tried to fulfil every dream of ours, but that does not mean that he has spoilt us. Both he and Maa were particular that though doing well in studies was important, good behaviour and a courteous code of conduct should be the topmost priority. They were very clear that they should never be called to school to ever have to discuss any bad behaviour on our part. And this rule became the cornerstone of our lives. As we grew older, we understood that since we were the children of a renowned personality, people were observing us carefully all the time. Abba ensured that our *taleem* was not just confined to the 'music room'. He would teach us about life, music and morality anywhere and everywhere he found the time. Sometimes we were even given lessons in the plane or at the London tube station! Whenever anything relevant to our upbringing came to Abba's mind, he shared it with us regardless of people around. For Abba, we have been the world around him.

Just as Abba had felt when he had moved to Delhi from Gwalior in 1957, when we were in school, we also felt that we had to make friends with those who understood our musical heritage. Like Abba, there were times when we too felt different to the other students around us. However, we learnt to be patient and tolerant. And as time passed, we did make our share of friends who understood our musical needs. Abba never insisted on us excelling at our studies. His abiding

desire was that we play to our optimal levels in the music room. While he took charge of our musical training, Abba left it to Maa to take care of the rest – the habits we developed, our studies, other activities, relationships, and so on. Maa was and still is the pillar of our house. Whenever, as children, we felt sad or low, Maa helped us to restore our self-confidence and face the world. She always emphasized the great lineage that we belonged to and encouraged us to make our father proud of us.

Abba has always credited Maa for being such a dedicated wife and mother. In turn she believed that her immense love for dance would always remain in her heart regardless of whether or not she physically performed on stage. Even today Maa strongly feels that her love for the fine arts shines through her husband and her two sons.

Maa has been Abba's official designer all these years (see overleaf too).

All the beautiful kurtas that he is well known for wearing are her creations. Maa keeps designing all the time for Abba and now, for both of us.

'Sarod for Harmony',
Carnegie Hall, New York,
23 May, 2000.

Temenos Academy,
St. James Palace,
London, 1997.

Barbican Centre,
London, July 1997.

Carnegie Hall, New York,
13 September, 1997.

Worn at Siri Fort
Auditorium, New Delhi, Nov.
2001. A 25th wedding
anniversary gift from us.

Angarakha – *styled kurta, designed*
by Maa, worn at photo shoot, 2001.

The common love for music that brought Maa and Abba together continues to remain the food of their life. For Maa's fiftieth birthday, Abba invoked a raga in her honour to demonstrate his enormous love and regard for her, and his appreciation of how she had sacrificed her career for her family. The raga was named *Subhalakshmi*, and was released in 1995 in an album called *To My Wife Subhalakshmi* by HMV. In fact, the raga was not only a tribute to Maa, but to all those women who have sacrificed their lives for their families.

Dadi Ammi's unexpected death took place the same year. On 30 May 1995, we were in London for a concert when we received the shocking news.

Abba's belief in gender equality and respect for women is reflected in his insistence that a child should always be known by the names of both parents. As a rule, therefore, we always mention Maa's name along with Abba's at all our concerts. Abba handed over the care of the three men in our family to Maa. She is the organiser, and handles all the correspondence and arrangements for our concerts. She designs the gorgeous kurtas that Abba and we wear at our concerts. To her, colours and music go together. 'I hear well when I dress well', is her often heard refrain. Her amazing sense of aesthetics results in the stage design often being conceived by her at our concerts. Her sensitivity as an artist is alert to the fact that in a concert, the ambience inspires the performer and the audience enormously – hence, the emphasis on clothes and the stage.

Maa is the disciplinarian in our family and Abba is our *trump card*. However, despite his soft and mellow personality, Abba has always felt strongly about certain things in life. His views are often hard to change or influence. It is because of these bold views that our life took a certain path. In 1988, our house was undergoing major renovations. To ensure that our education was not disrupted by this reconstruction, Abba and Maa decided to send us to Scindia School, a boarding school in Gwalior. This was the first time we had left home and the step was a break from our family tradition. As time passed, Abba began to miss us immensely. Maa missed us as well, but she was

Black *sherwani* with shawl worn at a photo shoot for Abba's album called *Sarod Mantra*, 2001.

Abba was not happy wearing the shawl, but agreed after some insistence.

more practical and contained her emotions. Abba came to meet us every week, telling Maa that he had work in Gwalior. He was also apprehensive that our *sarod*-playing would suffer, and, therefore, either came himself or sent his disciples to monitor our progress. On one occasion he sent his disciple Sriram Umrekar to Scindia School with a tape recorder to record us playing on a tape. When we received the tape from Sriram Umrekar, instead of recording our music on it, we put in a message to Maa and Abba – 'Why did you leave us here? We were so happy together, we want to come home.' On hearing the tape Maa and Abba felt terrible. Abba decided to make yet another 'sneaky trip' to Gwalior. On that trip, after taking special permission from the school authorities, he brought us back with him to Delhi. Though Maa was a little upset with Abba over his clandestine act (!) she could not hide her joy at seeing us back. From the next day onwards, we went back to good old Modern School! Abba's strong belief that our *sarod*-playing would suffer if we were not physically close to him, was the clincher in his decision to bring us home. If he had not brought us back home in 1988, who is to say we would have been playing the *sarod* today or be so close to both our parents.

Maa greeting Abba on the Assamese New Year, 13 April 2001.

A photo quietly taken by Amaan on the Assamese New Year as Maa touched Abba's feet as a mark of respect.

FACING PAGE:

A perfect couple.

Footprints in the Sands of Time

Lives of great men remind us
We can make our lives sublime.
And, departing, leave behind us
Footprints in the sands of time.

– Henry Wordsworth Longfellow

One thing that Abba has never taken for granted is his music. Be it the killing cold of a December morning or a humid afternoon, for Abba, there is no compromise as far as the *sarod* is concerned. His musical journey has been a very private one. He has given far more expression to the *sarod* – a new dimension. Initially, *sarod* players could elicit only single notes and double strokes from the instrument. After Abba made certain modifications to his style of playing, he could make the *sarod* produce an array of single notes, single strokes (*ekhera taans*), and unimaginably speedy *taans*. His contribution to the contemporary style of *sarod*-playing has added new meaning to compositions; he started playing ragas such as *Rageshwari, Saraswati, Bhupali* and *Hansdhoni* that had never been played on the *sarod* before. The *sarod* is a fretless instrument and thus, the movement in such ragas makes it hard for them to be played on the *sarod*. This innovation was a magnificient feat!

Today, Abba has the proud distinction of having influenced the style of various other string instrumentalists. Another unique

FACING PAGE:

Abba smiles on stage.

It is so difficult to make Abba give a natural smile when he is being photographed. He becomes so conscious! All of us have a tough time making him laugh naturally. Here Abba was caught unawares and was in a world of his own on stage.

79

Abba in concert.

Chatur Lal on the tabla and Abba's student, Rafi Ahemad on the tanpura. *1961.*

feature in Abba's playing is that he is perhaps one of the only musicians to play a complete composition. 'Complete' implies playing the *sthayee* (first part) and the *antara* (second part, upper octave portion). Historic and contemporary recordings of the *sarod* support this fact. The famous Indian classical vocalist, Pandit Bhimsen Joshi, remarked in the documentary entitled *Divya Drishti,* made on Abba: 'The *sarod* belongs to Ustad Amjad Ali Khan and Ustad Amjad Ali Khan belongs only to the *sarod*'.

Even though in the 1960s, Abba was one of the youngest performing artistes, he became one of the first musicians in the history of India classical music to perform solo evening concerts. Earlier on musicians usually participated in music festivals also known as Conferences in order to display their talents. By introducing the Western concept of solo evenings, Abba was able to interact personally with his beloved audience. He got love and good wishes in plentiful from his listeners and fans.

He was ready to face hardships and undertake extensive travelling to establish his reputation. He performed at many cultural events in Uttar Pradesh, Bihar, Madhya Pradesh, Maharashtra, Bengal and Tamil Nadu, among others. During his tours, Abba did have to face some power politics with senior instrumentalists who were just not ready to accept the fact that Abba had become an *ustad* at a young age, and was, therefore, their contemporary. However, concentrating on his love for the *sarod*, Abba managed to tide over these petty problems with humility. As a result of his determination to succeed, the 1960s saw the rise of a promising young *sarod* player who managed to play duets with various senior musicians.

Accompanying a delegation of dancers and musicians from New Delhi, Abba made his first overseas tour to the United States in 1963. It was extremely difficult for him to persuade Dada Abba to give him

Abba and Kishan Maharaj, Nagpur 1966.

Abba and Kishan Maharaj had been playing since the early '60s, but strangely, their first album together was released only in 1995.

permission because Dada Abba was uncomfortable with the idea of air travel. Moreover, Abba was Dada Abba's only hope in carrying his musical lineage forward, and Abba's well-being was a source of constant worry to him. After a lot of perseverance, Abba finally got the green signal to go on the trip. On his return, he was overwhelmed to see that his father had come to receive him at the airport.

Abba's love of the tabla enabled him to add new musical dimensions to his art. He introduced diversity into his recitals by playing with a wide range of tabla players including Ustad Habibuddin Khan, Ustad Alla Rakha Khan, Ustad Keramat Khan, Pandit Kanai Dutt and Ustad Latif Ahemad Khan. During the '60s and '70s, Abba was accompanied mostly by the famous tabla players Pandit Kishan Maharaj and Pandit Shamta Prasad.

Although Abba remained extremely particular about the sensitivities of his seniors, he managed to introduce some fun into his performances with them. One of his favourite stories relates to a performance in 1967 with Pandit Kishan Maharaj in Mauritius. The day was Janmashtami, coincidentally also Pandit Kishan Maharaj's birthday. Abba was in a jovial mood and decided to play a light trick

Ravi Shankar and Alla Rakha Khan after Abba's concert. 1960s, Kolkata.

on Pandit Kishan Maharaj. He told the organizers of the concert that it was his birthday too. As a result, along with Pandit Kishan Maharaj, he also ended up getting a lot of birthday presents. Of course, Abba and Pandit Kishan Maharaj distributed the presents equally amongst themselves, but first they had a good laugh!

A major milestone in Abba's professional life occurred in 1971. On his *actual* twenty-sixth birthday, Abba took the bold decision to play a solo, night-long concert at Kala Mandir Auditorium in Kolkata. The concert lasted for over nine hours and was attended by over one thousand people. Abba played five ragas that night: *Behag, Darbari Kanada, Shahana, Suhag Bhairav* and *Bhairavi* (on public demand). He played the first three ragas with Pandit Kishan Maharaj and the last two with Ustad Keramat Khan. With this, he became the first ever known Indian classical musician to perform alone for an entire night.

Some years later, he gave his second all-night concert on 30 April 1977 at Rabindra Sadan Auditorium in Kolkata. This time his moral support came from closer quarters – Maa. The concert was sold out long before the day of the performance. However, on the day itself, hundreds of people without tickets appeared to hear Abba play. Not

Abba with Prime Minister Indira Gandhi.

Receiving the Padma Shri at the age of 29 in 1975 at Rashtrapati Bhawan. Abba has been one of the youngest ever recipients of a civilian award.

Abba, Arup Kumar Sarkar
and Ali Akbar Khan.

*Taken during the Haafiz Ali
Khan Music festival in Kolkata
in 1977. This was yet another
memorable festival. It went on
for over six days.*

wanting to pass up the golden opportunity of hearing Ustad Amjad
Ali Khan, these music lovers broke open the doors of the auditorium.
Abba, who had already taken center-stage by then, realized that he
had a stampede on his hands. In an attempt to calm the restless
audience, he announced on the mike that he would wait patiently
and not begin the concert until the ushers had accommodated all the
people in the auditorium. For fear of being caught underfoot in case
of a stampede, the ushers removed their badges and merged with the
audience. During the concert, there were people all around the stage,
in the aisles and in the wings. Abba's solo performance of three ragas
lasted for over eight hours. When it ended, people clamoured for
more. The first raga Abba played was *Yaman* with Sabir Khan who

Abba and Michael Nyman, the pianist.

This picture was taken at the Royal Festival Hall, London, at a concert held in aid of the Gujarat earthquake victims in February 2001.

was appearing for the first time in Kolkata on the tabla; the second was *Bageshwari* with Pandit Shankar Ghosh on the tabla; and the third, *Anand Bharav* with Pandit Shamta Prasad.

During the 1970s, besides performing in concerts all over India, Abba travelled overseas frequently. He performed at the Prague Festival in erstwhile Czechoslovakia; the Shiraz Festival in Iran; for UNESCO in Switzerland, where he received the UNESCO Award (Lord Yehudi Menuhin was present to hear him), and at other venues such as Queen Elizabeth Hall in London, and all over the US. By the grace of God, the hard work that he had put into establishing his career in the 1960s and 1970s was finally beginning to show results. The 1980s and 1990s proved to be glorious years for Abba. During this

Abba at the Haafiz Ali Khan
Festival in New Delhi.

*Kumar Bose accompanies him
on the tabla, with his students,
Sharafat Khan and Bishwajeet
Roy Chaudhury on the* tanpura.

FACING PAGE:

Abba files his nails.

*Western audiences often find this
amusing, but it is necessary
while playing.*

period, he became an international figure, representing India in
Geneva at the First World Arts Summit. He had the honour of being
the first Indian Visiting Professor at the University of Yorkshire, and
performed in concerts all over the globe. Several recitals were held at
the Royal Albert Hall and Royal Festival Hall in London, the Carnegie
Hall in New York, the Kennedy Center in Washington D.C., the
Theatre de la Ville in Paris, the opera house in Sydney and the
Santury Hall in Japan. In fact, he was the first Indian musician to play
at the Santury Hall. During these celebrated years, he collaborated
with Russian violinist Igor Frolov, soprano Glenda Simpson, guitarist

Abba and Shamta Prasad at a private concert in New Delhi at the Belgium Embassy in the early '70s.

Barry Mason and the British cellist Mathew Barley. He composed a piece for the Hong Kong Philharmonic Orchestra titled *Tribute to Hong Kong*. Yoshikazu FuKuMura conducted this piece. The list of Abba's achievements from this period onwards is endless.

At the request of various organisers, Abba has, over the years, played duets with a wide spectrum of Indian musicians from both the Hindustani and the Carnatak systems of Indian classical music. He has give recitals with, the *veena* maestros Emani Shankar Shastri, Doreswami Srinivas Iyengar; violinists Pandit V.G. Jog, M.S. Gopalakrishnan, Lalgudi G. Jayaraman ; sitarists Imrat Khan and Rais Khan; the great vocalist Srimati Girja Devi, and the violist

88

Abba playing at his 26th birthday concert.

Held in Kolkata in 1971, this concert made him the first and only musician to play an all-night concert by himself that went on for over nine hours. Kishan Maharaj plays the tabla.

Abba and Zakir Hussain, New Delhi, 1985.

Abba has always come forward to support charitable organizations and the needy. This concert was held in aid of the Bhopal Gas tragedy victims.

FACING PAGE:

Abba at his best.

We have seen people coming to Abba after concerts and weeping, being deeply affected by his music. Others get him flowers, food, gifts . . . and he is literally worshipped in certain places.

Dr Balamurli Krishna. In 1995, Abba turned fifty. Huge receptions were organized for him in London, New Delhi, Kolkata, Chennai, Mumbai and different parts of the United States.

As a result of his extensive contribution to the field of music, Abba has received various awards and honours. The first award that was bestowed on him was the Sarod Samrat at the age of fifteen. Amongst other prestigious awards and titles Abba has received are the UNESCO Award, the Crystal Award by the World Economic Forum in Davos in February 1997, Unicef's National Ambassadorship, and an honorary doctorate by York University. He is one of the few Indians to receive all three *Padma* Awards: the *Padma Shri* in 1974, the *Padma Bhushan* in 1991, the *Padma Vibhushan* in 2001, and just recently, the *Deshikottama* – honorary doctorate by the Vishva Bharati University in Shantiniketan.

Even while Abba's reputation as a *sarod* virtuoso was growing swiftly, he ensured that his accompanists were equally involved in the limelight that was bestowed upon him. He also made a special

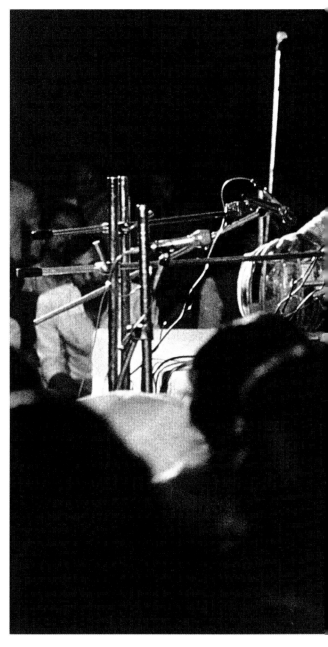

Abba playing the tabla.

Abba would often play the tabla for us while teaching us. He has been very deeply interested in the tabla since he was a child. His associations with a wide range of percussionists confirms this.

PAGES 92-93:

Abba in an overcrowded concert hall, early '80s.

Kumar Bose accompanies Abba on the tabla. It is a tradition in India for the listeners to sit around the platform and on the stage at times when there are no seats left in the hall. This makes for a very different kind of rapport between the artiste and music lovers.

Abba during an orchestra rehearsal in Kolkata, 1995.

Abba has composed music for several orchestras with his students and other young musicians. Seen here are Tanmoy Bose (front row), Abba's frequent accompanist; his disciples Sudeshana Bhattacharya and Shunondo Mukerjee are seen on the sarod *in the second row*

effort to promote young artists and launch new talents. He has been responsible for introducing and guiding famous artistes and numerous tabla players who continue to accompany him even today. Since he is well acquainted with the art of playing the tabla, he is able to extract optimal levels of performances from his accompanists. Some of the tabla players that Abba has encouraged over the years are Shafaat Ahemad Khan, Rashid Mustafa, Subhash Nirwan, Sukhvindar Singh Namdhari, Kumar Bose, Jayanta Bose, Ananda Gopal, Sudir Pandey, Mithelesh Kumar Jha, Chandra Mohan, Fateh Singh Gangani and Tanmoy Bose.

Through the years, he has consciously tried to impart his musical legacy to disciples from various realms of life. He has trained and presented a range of pupils in major music festivals year after year. He has even supported some of his disciples financially. Amongst some of his close disciples are Ashit Ghatak, Shubhani Sarkar, Rupam Ghosh, Pratap Shau, Narendra Nath Dhar, Shunondo Mukerjee, Sudeshena Bhattacharjee, Rafi Ahemad Khan, Rakesh Prassana, Deepa Ranganathan, Raja Ray, Indrek Roy, Kamal Reddy, Abhik Sarkar, Chakrapani Singh, Saroj Ghosh, Subhash Ghosh, Sharafat Khan, S. Kalidas, Bishwajit Roy Chowdhury, Abdulla Azam, Daud Sadozai, Praful Kelkar, Paul, Benjamin, John Ale, Prabhat Mukerjee, Pramod Shankar, Shoba Deepak Singh, Mukesh Sharma, Mithelesh Kumar Jha, Anupriya Sharma, Avantika Keswani, Ravi Pawar, Hariom Dubey, Sanjay Sharma, Kari Dubey, Biseswar Sen, Sunil Saxena, Iqbal Narodh, Dev Shankar, Jyoti Shankar, Shalil Gustad, Debajoyti Bose, Guru Dev Singh, Harbajan Singh, Varun Narayan and hopefully – both of us.

As a guru, Abba has never discriminated between the musical education that he has imparted to his sons and his other disciples. There is nothing that he has taught us that he has not taught his other disciples. Despite his immeasurable affection for his students, he has, however, at times felt that after achieving professional eminence, some of them have turned their backs on him. Abba has

Abba teaching his students.

FOLLOWING PAGES 100-101:

Abba with Girja Devi at a concert in Kolkata.

Girja Devi ties a raakhi *on Abba – the sacred thread a sister ties on her brother's wrist in Kolkata, 1996.*

95

ROYAL PARTY ON TOUR

From: The Lady-in-Waiting to H.R.H. The Princess of Wales

14th February, 1992

Dear Th Ali Khan,

The Princess of Wales has asked me to thank you for so kindly giving her your very old and beautiful shawl after The Prime Minister's dinner.

Her Royal Highness was so grateful to you for lending it to her and very touched by your generosity in parting with it and it will be a marvellous memento of her happy time in India.

Again thank you and The Princess asks me to send her very best wishes.

Yours sincerely,

Laura Lonsdale

Mrs. James Lonsdale

Ustad Amjad Ali Khan

never expected any material or financial returns for his teaching. The only expectation that he has had is that they continue to show him trust and respect even after they have launched out on their own. It has saddened him that some have overlooked this courtesy and put aside the sanctity of the *guru-shishya parampara*. In 1992, during Abba's tour of the Far East, a sitar player who had been Abba's disciple since the 1960s, informed Abba that he had recently become a renowned sitar guru in Singapore. He also indicated that since he had now acquired a high standing in the musical circle of Singapore, he expected Abba to interact with him according to his newly acquired status. Abba was disheartened to see that a guru's blessings no longer counted for anything. There is the case of another disciple who, after having learnt from Abba for over ten years, has constantly made blatant and derogatory remarks (directly or indirectly) about Abba in well-known newspapers such as *The Times of India* and *The Pioneer*. Abba is especially pained because in his musical upbringing, the fact that any disciple would make adverse comments about his guru was unheard of.

Abba, Lady Diana, Prince Charles and Maa.

At a dinner held in the Prime Minister's house in New Delhi in 1992, Abba got a message on his table that Lady Diana was feeling cold. He went over immediately and put his shawl around her. She wore it the entire evening. When she wanted to return the antique jamewar shawl, Abba asked her to accept it as a small gift from India.

Abba presenting his disciples at the Guru Shishya Parampara Festival, New Delhi, 1985.

Left to right: Abba, Sunil Saxena, Sriram Umrekar, Sanjay Sharma, Debjyoti Bose, Abhik Sarkar..

Musical interchange, New Delhi, 1989.

Abba and Ravi Shankar switch instruments with each other and share a lighter moment. Both their gurus learnt from Ustad Wazir Khan.

Yet another distressing memory is that of a *sarod* player, who was Abba's disciple since the 1970s. This youngster was Abba's only disciple who had the fortune of residing in his guru's house, as well as constantly being around the musical legacy he wanted to adopt. During this time, it was brought to Abba's attention that his disciple had been behaving in an unseemly manner with some of his female acquaintances. Abba was and still is a person who has always maintained that in any situation, the respect given to a woman is all important. On hearing about this undesirable behaviour of one of his dearest disciples, Abba advised him to return to his family in Kolkata. The latter began telling everyone that Abba had asked him to leave his house because he was intimidated by his disciple's professional progress. When Abba heard the comments that his *shishya* was

Abba, guitarist Barry Mason and soprano Glenda Simpson.

All three rehearsing together before their concert together, 1990.

101

Lord Yehudi Menuhin hugs Abba.

After Abba's concert at the World Economic Forum in Davos, 1997, Abba and Lord Menuhin gave a talk on music the next day.

FACING PAGE FROM TOP TO BOTTOM:

Abba and Richard Gere 2001; Abba with Vilayat Khan, Princeton 1996; Abba and Kishan Maharaj, Benares, 1993.

making, he was shocked that a disciple could even think that a guru would ever be envious of a disciple's success. To make matters worse, he also got to know that this disciple's father had been a student of Dada Abba's, and had never come to see him, unlike all other students of his father's. To add insult to injury, another friend and disciple of Abba offered patronage to the errant disciple in her music institute located in New Delhi.

Yet another case is that of a *sarod* player who currently resides in Israel and was Abba's disciple for over fifteen years. On one occasion, in an attempt to dissuade Abba from making a trip to Israel, he told him that his performance would not be commercially viable there! Then there are two artistes: a *sarod* player who assisted Abba in a composition for UNICEF's fortieth anniversary, and a violinist, who was Abba's disciple for over fourteen years, both of who, with Abba's permission, used the name Ustad Amjad Ali Khan for an academy that would propagate the cause of Indian classical music. However, after the academy received large donations from music lovers, the young *sarod* player and violinist decided to use these contributions for their personal advantage and, simultaneously broke off their association with Abba. This was connivance of the worst kind.

Despite these bitter experiences, Abba still continues to teach new disciples without any financial consideration. Had he been a little hard hearted, maybe such episodes would not have hurt him as much. Anyhow, he has continued to maintain that the limelight must be shared with young disciples.

As we grew older, there came a time in Abba's career when he decided to share his sacred stage with us as he had done with his other disciples. When we first appeared on stage with him, our launch was very matter of fact. He did not wish to use his clout or our ancestry as a publicity tool; he wanted us to earn our place in the hearts of listeners solely on merit. We believe that when Abba allowed us to share centre-stage with him, a new dimension was added to his

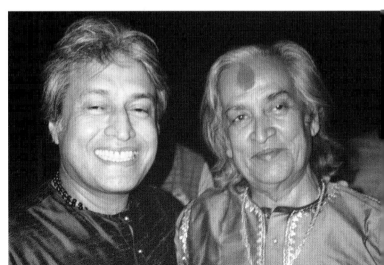

103

recitals, which now featured two generations. We have so far performed some memorable concerts together, and given some unforgettable recitals abroad at Carnegie Hall in New York, Royal Festival Hall in London, Palais Beaux-Arts in Brussels, the Kennedy Center in Washington D.C., the High Grove Estate of His Royal Highness Prince Charles and, of course, all the performances that we have ever given anywhere in India.

Abba has always maintained that only a good human being can be a good musician. Thus, he has constantly made an honest effort to do his bit for the less privileged. He has performed for various philanthropic organizations and causes all over the country and the world – UNICEF, The Spastic Society, The Cancer Society, The Blind Relief Fund, being a few such organizations.

Abba's quest for professional and personal perfection constantly makes him look for opportunities to better himself and reach out to others.Undoubtedly, his greatness is still to come.

The Human Being:
Face to Face

One gets from life what one gives to it.

– Indira Gandhi

Professionally Abba is today acknowledged as an icon of Indian classical music across the globe. Despite his widespread fame, he continues to remain a humble person. He believes that there is still a lot more he needs to discover about the *sarod*. In order to enhance his understanding of, and relationship with the instrument, he has developed a personal relationship with each of his *sarods*, naming each of them. His favourite one is called Ganga. It is Maa's favourite as well because its creation coincided with their marriage. Abba's other *sarods* are Jamuna, Brahmaputra, Saaz and Godavari. Abba refers to his personal interaction with the *sarod* as musical flirtation. Other *sarods* that he has used in his lifetime are displayed and preserved at the Sarod Ghar in Gwalior, alongside the instruments of his ancestors.

Abba's credibility as a musician has not been established without constant enrichment of character. He has always taught us that professional accomplishments are futile unless a man remains humble even after he receives eminence. His naturally modest personality can be attributed to his disciplined upbringing, lessons taught by life itself and the constant process of contemplation that he is perpetually engaged in.

A God-fearing person, Abba believes that the act of praying must not be confined to a church, temple, or mosque: 'God may not always

FACING PAGE:

A God-fearing person, Abba believes in the religion of love and humanity.

107

Maa, Abba and Amaan at the Dargarh of Khwaja Moin-ud-Din Chisti at Ajmer.

Our parents have always kept an open-minded attitude towards all religions. Consequently all sacred places hold an attraction for us, irrespective of the religion, place or location.

BOTTOM:

Abba being honoured by Mother Teresa.

Abba had great regard for Mother Teresa. In 1999, he released an album called Tribute to Mother Teresa.

be present in every man-made structure, but he is constantly present in every man's soul'. Not one to discriminate among different religions, he believes in the religion of love and humanity. Maintaining the ideology that God dwells in a man's heart, Abba prays wherever and whenever he wants. His secular outlook has guided his footsteps to temples, mosques, shrines and *dargahs* all over the world. He considers himself fortunate to have been able to do so. He is a frequent visitor to the *dargah* of Khwaja Moin-un-din-Shah Chisti at Ajmer; Hazrat Qutubuddin Aulia, Hazrat Amir Khusro, Hazrat Nizammuddin Aauliya, and Matka Shah Pir in New Delhi; Hazrat Sabir Saheb in Roorkee; Baba Haji Ali in Mumbai; the Sabrimalai Temple in Kerala; Tirupathi Temple in Andhra Pradesh; Shirdi Temple in Maharasthra, and, of course, cathedrals all over the world. During his trip to Iraq, he had the good fortune of visiting Hazrat Ali's *dargah*.

Although Abba believes in only one supreme power unseen by man, he respects holy men all over the world. He has received the blessings of many, such as His Holiness the Dalai Lama, who has even attended Abba's recitals on numerous occasions. His Holiness also launched the World Festival of Sacred Music in New Delhi in May 1999. Abba held Mother Teresa in very high regard. After Mother Teresa renounced the world in September 1997, Abba was heartbroken. The same year he released an album called *Tribute to Mother Teresa* to honour the great Mother. In 1989, the famous singer of southern India, Shrimati M.S. Subbulakshmi, arranged for our family to pay a musical tribute to the Shankracharya Chandrashekhar Saraswati (Maha Periavar) of Kanchi Kamakotu Peetam and Shankracharya Jayendra Saraswati. We performed in front of the Shankracharya Chandrashekhar Saraswati (Maha Periavar) in 1989. Abba believes that this performance will always remain a great blessing for him. Shri Satya Sai Baba is another revered mahatma who has blessed our family. We have performed several times for his birthday celebrations in Puttaparthi, near Bangalore. Abba was also the first north Indian classical musician to perform at the samadhi of the South Indian saint-musician Thyagaraja. For this performance, as per the guidelines of the samadhi , Abba especially learnt a *krithi* or song-oriented composition of Thyagaraja.

As a part of his religious ideologies, Abba maintains that personal adjustments are essential to nurture harmonious surroundings. In his eyes, the ability to make personal adjustments is a form of prayer in itself. For example, in our family there are four of us living together. At times, our personalities are bound to clash. According to Abba, when this happens, the ability of a family member to modify his

Abba and HH The Dalai Lama at the launch of the World Festival of Sacred Music, 2000.

'When Amjad Ali Khan performs, he carries with him a deep human spirit, a warm feeling and a sense of caring.'
– HH The Dalai Lama.

109

Abba in his role as UNICEF's National Ambassador.

Abba has a very old association with UNICEF. In fact on its fortieth anniversary, Abba composed a musical piece titled Ekta Se Shanti performed by an orchestra of children.

current frame of mind in order to incorporate the demands of other family members (and thereby avoid a conflict), is a form of prayer. We have had the good fortune of being a close-knit household because all the members in our family have been able to actuate this principle of Abba's. An amusing aspect of our family disagreements (whenever there are any) is that Abba closes the windows of his bedroom to prevent the neighbours from listening to what is going on. This, unfortunately, has the reverse effect, and we flare up all the more!

A generous nature is part and parcel of Abba's personality. As long as the demands are within his wide-ranging ideological parameters, seldom or practically never has he ever said No to us for anything! Since Maa was a disciplinarian, Abba turned into our trump card when we were children. He pampered us by buying us ice cream whenever we wanted; he would help to get a day off from school, and would buy us all the toys we badgered him for. Even in his dealings with people who are not family, Abba has always been kind hearted and prayed for their well-being. Whenever we pass the Breach Candy Hospital in Mumbai or The All India Institute of Medical Sciences in New Delhi, or for that matter, any other hospital, he prays for the quick recovery of all the patients in the hospital.

There is another side to Abba that very few people are aware of. He has a subtle sense of humour, which is very contagious. Once, during one of our concert tours in UK, we were taking a stroll with Abba down Oxford Street in London. We decided to go into a music store. Abba wasn't too keen on going inside, so he decided to wait outside while we went in, giving us all the

money he was carrying. When we finished our purchases and came out, we saw him eating an ice cream. It struck us that since he had given all his money to us, he could not have had any money to pay for the ice cream. He must have been given a free treat, and that too, from a tight-lipped Londoner! The next day, we were walking down Oxford Street again and this time Maa happened to be with us. We came across the same vendor who had given Abba a free ice cream the previous day. When the man saw Abba he said, 'You again!' Abba laughed out loud, pointed to Maa and said to the man: 'Look! This time I've brought my bank along with me.' Even though Abba insisted on paying for his purchase, the ice cream vendor gave him yet another free ice cream! From that time on, each time we saw the ice-cream man, Abba and he exchanged a hearty smile.

Much to Maa's embarrassment, with Abba around, episodes like this keep occurring from time to time. On another tour abroad, Abba's love for feeding birds actually resulted in a public signboard being put up in London. Abba bought a loaf of bread and went to Victoria Street to feed the pigeons. While he was feeding them, a policeman came and told him to stop immediately. When the

TOP LEFT:

Abba and Raffle.

Raffle was our Labrador who was with us for a few years. As we were travelling a lot, he was being neglected. Hence, we gave him away to our close family relations after some time.

TOP RIGHT:

Abba feeding birds in London.

Abba is the man responsible for the board erected near Victoria Station that says, 'Do not feed birds'.

policeman left, Abba remarked '*Kitna battameez aadmi hai* (What an ill-mannered man)'. A few months later, when both of us were in London on a tour for the Asian Music Circuit, we saw a big board saying PLEASE DO NOT FEED THE BIRDS on Victoria Street. Perhaps the signboard had been put up courtesy Abba's default! His love for birds is deep. Apparently Dada Abba used to tell him that religious saints reincarnate as pigeons after they renounce the world, and that is why they are always seen in places of worship. For years now, in our house, food and water has been left for the birds on the terrace every morning. Many times, Abba offers the food and water himself. Of course, he has been known to put out an entire week's quota out on one day itself! If he is travelling abroad and calls us from overseas, he always makes it a point to ask if *bajra* has been fed to the pigeons or not.

LEFT:

New York, 1997.

Earlier, Abba wore trousers, suits and shirts frequently but for the last ten or fifteen years, he has preferred to wear only kurtas. We do, however, force him to wear Western clothes, to which he grudgingly agrees.

TOP:

New York, 1986.

Abba started playing tennis quite often during his US tour in 1986. He even got us great tennis racquets when he came back.

Abba's famous yellow
Mercedes, Germany 1978.

*He had a great attachment to
this car. It was his third love
after his sarod and Maa. He had
sleepless nights when the car
was in the driveway.*

Abba's love for birds emanates from his love for nature. He has always loved to go on long walks, especially in areas surrounded by greenery. However, given the hectic pace of his life, he does not get much time to indulge his passion. When we are overseas, he makes it a point to take the time out and go on extensive walks through various parks. After his love for birds and greenery comes his love for horses. He truly admires their structure, grace and beauty. Our house is filled with objets d'art on horses. However he does not fancy horse racing. Eating good food is another of Abba's passions. He enjoys eating fresh salad at least half an hour before his main meal and insists that we do the same. He appreciates cuisine from different parts of the world, his only dislike being the extensive use of flour in his food. What he does have a weakness for is extremely rich food such as *parathas*, *malai* and *korma*, but he manages to exercise great self-control. He knows exactly how much he wants to eat and should eat. Come what may, however delicious the food, he does not exceed the limits that he has set for himself – he will not change his mind no matter how much one forces him to.

Some of his habits are hard to change though. Whenever a photo shoot takes place in our home, studio or outside, he ends up directing the photographer. His favourite instruction to the photographer is to sit and take his photograph. Somehow he feels his photograph comes out better that way! Till today Maa complains about Abba's pending paper work and his habit of writing down telephone numbers and addresses anywhere and everywhere – even in her diary. On one of his birthdays, we presented him with fancy chit pads – a whole lot of them. Although he now maintains a telephone diary, when he really needs an important number, he still looks for Maa's diary!

Abba's reputation for not being able to withhold surprises is well known. However, he did manage to keep Maa's fiftieth birthday party a surprise for her. Of course we co-hosted the party. It involved long planning for over six months. The noted singer Srimati Girja Devi sang on the occasion and Abba released an album, *To My Wife Subhalakshmi*, which was brought out by HMV. Maa did not have a clue about anything and was, therefore, greatly moved that day.

Maa's affectionate name for Abba is Amji. Over the years many friends of our parents have started calling him by this name. He, however, does not take kindly to this, feeling that only his wife has the right to do so. Of late, he has started fasting on various days which he calls his non-cereal days. Both of us joke that whenever there is a shortage of fruit in the market, you know that Abba is fasting. He is not amused by that though.

Trinidad, 1992.

Abba lost in himself at the Maracas beach in Trinidad.

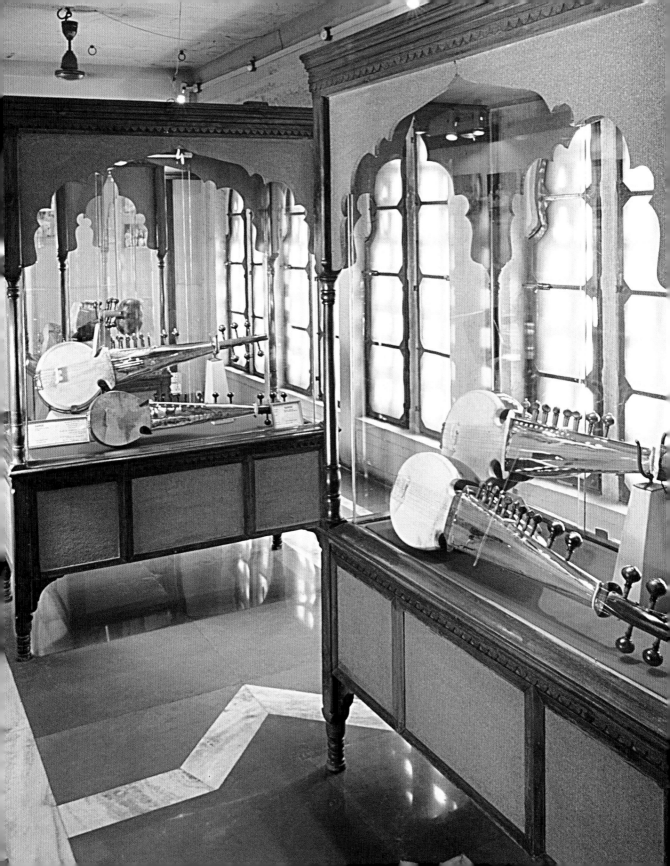

Giving Abba a birthday gift is a difficult proposition. He's just not interested in anything but music, and now the Sarod Ghar (Museum of Music) in Gwalior, his birthplace. Be it a fancy car or a designer watch, it's only if the family insists that he agrees to get one. Actually, he likes to keep a low profile and is always conscious of not drawing unnecessary attention to himself. However, there was a time when Abba did have a fascination for cars. Maa has told us how once, after having bought a very fine car from overseas, he would keep getting up in the middle of the night and look out of the bedroom window to check on the car standing in the driveway. Once he knew that all was well with his new baby, he would go back to a peaceful sleep.

Abba loves to surround himself with youngsters. He has an innate fondness for young people and he feels that in his interaction with us as a guru, he has learnt a lot about how to teach and interact

FACING PAGE AND TOP:

Sarod Ghar.

Over the years Abba has developed a very strong bonding with the Sarod Ghar – the museum in Gwalior and his ancestral home. Even when he is travelling, he is in constant touch with the staff there. He is concerned about the maintenance of his sarods and the other instruments that are displayed there. Every time he visits Gwalior, he spends the whole day in that historic house, reliving nostalgic memories.

Ancestral *Rabab*

In the 1700s, the rabab *was modified to the* sarod *in India by Ghulam Bandegi Khan Bangash, one of Abba's ancestors.*

Saaz, Abba's *sarod.*

The maker of the sarod *was Heman Sen.*

Abba's childhood sarod.

Played in the 1960s, this was made by Gopal & Sons.

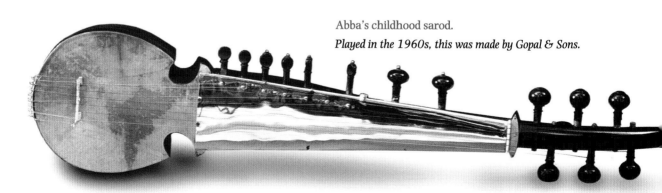

Ganga, Abba's *sarod*.

This sarod *and Maa and Abba's marriage go hand in hand as Ganga too came into Abba's life in 1976. Its maker was Heman Sen.*

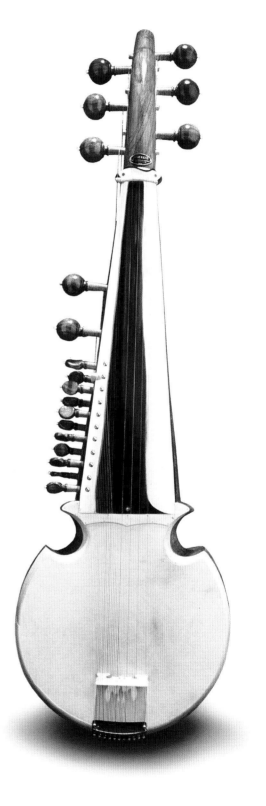

Abba's sarod, Brahamaputra.

This was also made by Heman Sen.

with them better. This makes our friends feel very comfortable around him. Sometimes he even shares stories about his younger days with them. Of course, his good looks still continue to break a million hearts, even arousing our envy at times!

In spite of usually being a polite person, people often misunderstand Abba, due to no real fault of his own. This has happened in our presence on occasion. A man was once talking to him very seriously about certain issues in life. After listening for a while, Abba started humming right in his face. One of us gave him a push under the table to make him stop. Musical thoughts come to him suddenly, and he forgets everything else!

The one thing that Abba cannot stand is *battameezi* or rude behaviour. He cannot stomach disrespect to the elderly. He believes in traditions like touching the feet of older people as a mark of respect, and feels extremely disheartened when he sees young people today rejecting such ancient Indian traditions and legacies. He decries casual and abrasive behaviour that is wrongly disguised as modernization. His message to young people today is that modernization is a wonderful thing as long as the Indian traditional values of humility, politeness and respect are retained.

A spontaneous person, Abba has broken out of set agendas on some occasions. When he was awarded an honorary doctorate by the University of Yorkshire in England, in the midst of his address he sang a few lines of *Raga Yaman* in honour of the famous soprano Dame Janet Baker, who presented him with the degree. This was the first time that a recipient of a doctorate sang in the Yorkshire University Convocation Hall. Everyone was taken aback and overwhelmed. Another time when he was the guest of honour at our concert at the French Embassy in New Delhi, 2001, in aid of the Gujarat earthquake victims, he agreed to play a short piece to be a part of the cause. He just appeared on stage unannounced, much to the delight of the audience and played two favourite songs of Mahatma Gandhi who also belonged to Gujarat. Such is the extent of Abba's spontaneity.

Abba with Prof. Cook, Vice Chancellor, University of York, England; Dame Janet Baker, Prof. Neil Sorrell, head of music department. Yorkhire, England, 1997.

After the convocation ceremony, a doctorate was conferred upon Abba by Dame Janet Baker. Abba gave a very moving speech and sang a few lines of Raga Yaman *as a tribute to Janet Baker, who is a soprano singer herself.*

A Father's Note

The night you were born, I ceased being my
father's boy and became my son's father.
That night I began a new life.

– Henry Gregor Felson

'I can't believe that my young sons, Amaan and Ayaan, who are still in their twenties, have written a book on me while I am still serving the world through my music. It is indeed a novel concept for them to share the life of their guru and father with the rest of the world. Perhaps, in keeping with today's time and age, it is an important and relevant aspect. No doubt children have a knack of noticing and questioning parents about life. However there are a few things they have not included which would be best written by me.

In our family, right from the beginning, kindness of heart has always been of prime importance. The humaneness of my father's character, his sincerity, his commitment to music and faith in God impressed me greatly as a child. 'Do unto others as you would have others do unto you' was his dictum. He also ingrained in me the reality that without faith in God, one could not become a great musician. My mother too was a kind-hearted and loving person, always distributing food, clothes and money to the needy.

I have been extremely fortunate to have a wife like Subhalakshmi, who is an artiste herself. She, therefore, understands my views and me. She has been a pillar of strength in my life, standing by me always. I believe that an artiste always remains an artiste, even if a non-performing one: the art lives on forever. In spite of coming from different backgrounds, our ideologies have nurtured a spirit of

FACING PAGE:

At home – a family well in tune with each other.

123

togetherness between us. We share the same feelings, equally feel the presence of God in our lives, commitment, discipline, and freedom of thought and expression. We have tried to inculcate the same in our sons from a very young age. Today we are happy to see that they are mature individuals with a tremendous sense of duty. While on their way to becoming good musicians, they are also aware of what is happening in the rest of the world. They are now free to make independent decisions regarding important aspects of their lives. I have never told them that classical music should be their profession; in fact I feel embarrassed to call it a profession – it is a way of life, a passion. I only hope that Amaan and Ayaan choose wives who will enable our sons to carry forward to their children, the tradition of humaneness that our family has followed.

A guru is one who shows his disciple the light in the darkness. The pupil must recognize the intentions of the guru and his feelings. Apart from the teachings of the guru, it is the vibrations, prayers, words and wisdom of the guru that are essential to a pupil's development. In my journey as a guru to Amaan and Ayaan, I have tried to teach them these ideologies along with music. It is also the onus of the pupil to show genuine integrity and honesty towards his teacher.

I have attempted to teach my sons the virtues of the *guru-shishya* relationship.I am happy and proud that both the brothers are on the right track. Since the two of them have different natures and ways of expressing themselves in music, when they play together, they make a good combination. The two of them should play solo at times, which they have started doing now.

My wife and I feel very proud and grateful to the people of our country and indeed, all over the world, for the love they have bestowed on us. Amaan and Ayaan still have to fulfil their destinies through their music. I pray that their music be filled with the fragrance of respect, grace, tradition, culture and Indianness. That would be a fitting contribution on their part to the world. I, for my part, only want to continue serving my country through my music.

At the holy Ganges, Kolkata, December 2001.

After visiting the Kali temple in Dakhineshwar, we walked near the Holy River Ganges overlooking the Howrah Bridge.

Ragas created by Abba

Abba never feels that a raga is created; he maintains that it is invoked. He treats every raga like a newborn baby. Therefore it is natural for the raga to have some association with its family members, and reflect flashes of some traditional ragas. Abba does not look upon a raga as a mere scale. He calls it an atman. He says, 'Every raga has a soul, and every musical note is the sound of God.' New faces (ragas) come to his mind and ask him their names; as they have no names, Abba names them and they become new ragas.

Listening to most of Abba's ragas, one feels that they are traditional ragas which were born thousands of years ago, but for some reasons, not discovered. Many of today's young musicians, including both of us, are playing these ragas.

What Abba says on his creations:

According to the theoretical aspect of North Indian classical music, every raga should usually have a vaadi *and* samvaadi *note. However, I feel that certain ragas cannot be explained through notation only. One needs to understand the character of each raga and understand its mood. Even the movement (chalan) of each raga can only be explained by* taleem. *This is the character of Indian classical music, where two plus two is not always four.*

Swar Sameer (1964)   *Evening raga*

I had initially called this Raga Mand Sameer. *However, not to confuse people with the folk* Maand, *I renamed it* Swar Sameer *in 1990. I first played this raga at the Harballabh Music Festival in Jalandar in Punjab. This raga was inspired by* Raga Rageshwari *and* Raga Joge.

Kiran Ranjani (1966)   *Evening raga*

The beauty of Raga Jhinjhoti, Pilu *and* Shiv Ranjani *inspired me enormously. This raga is a tribute to them.*

Chandra Dhwani (1968)   *Evening raga*

I premiered this raga in Kolkata in 1968 at Nishit Sangeet Sammelan. It was an inspiration from the haunting Raag Kaushik Dhwani, Khammaj *and* Raag Rageshwari. *This raga emerged at a very special moment in my life.*

Hari Priya Kanada (1970s)   *Night raga*

This raga is a tribute to Swami Haridas, who was the guru of Mian Tansen. I performed this raga at the Music Festival held in his memory in Brindavan. Inspired by the Carnatic raga, Raga Charukesi, *I have given it a structure of the Kannada family of ragas.*

Suhaag Bhairav (1971)   *Morning raga*

I played Suhaag Bhairav *for the first time in Kolkata at my first all-night concert.* Raga Ramkeli, Bhatyar *and* Bhairav *inspired me.* Suhag Bhairav *sounds like a sad story about the sufferings of a romantic couple.*

Amiri Todi (1974)   *Morning raga*

After the sad demise of Ustad Amir Khan Saheb, I performed this raga on his first death anniversary. We had really spent some beautiful moments together and I was really saddened by his death. This raga was inspired by Raga Bilaskhani Todi *and* Raga Shahana, *both favourites of the legendary Ustad Amir Khan.*

Lalita Dhwani (1976)   *Evening raga*

This raga was inspired by Raga Lalit *and* Raga Kaushik Dhwani. *I first played it in Benaras in 1976. It was recorded live by Navras Records as part of my fiftieth birthday concert in London at the Royal Festival Hall.*

Shyam Shri (1980)   *Evening raga*

I played this raga at the Teen Murti House in New Delhi in 1980 on the death anniversary of Pandit Jawaharlal Nehru. This was recorded live by HMV. If this raga is played as a straight scale, than it is Raga Latangi of the Carnatic system of classical music. However, in this case, the treatment is very different.

Saraswati Kalyan (1980s)   *Evening raga*

This raga was inspired by Ragas Saraswati and Yaman Kalyan. In the Carnatic system this scale is called Raga Vachaspati, but I have given it my own interpretation.

Priyadarshani (1984)   *Evening raga*

Smt Indira Gandhi's tragic death made me recall some beautiful moments I had spent with her. This new face emerged in my mind. The Rajasthani Maand, Raga Kaushik Dhwani and Raga Poorvi inspired this raga.

Shivanjali (1987)   *Evening raga*

First played at the Festival of India, in Moscow, 1987, this raga emerged while I was travelling in Russia, listening to Russian songs. But, technically, it is an inspiration from Raag Kafi Kanada, Malkauns and Darbari Kanada.

Jawahar Manjari (1990)   *Evening raga*

This raga was first played in London in the presence of Prince Charles. It was Pandit Jawaharlal Nehru's birthday, and incidentally, that of Prince Charles too. It is my humble tribute to Pandit Nehru whom I met several times with my father, and was inspired by Raga Kedar, Raga Anandi and Raga Rageshwari.

Mangresh (1990)   *Evening raga*

I was to perform in Mumbai at the death anniversary of Pandit Dinanath Mangeshkar, the father of Lata Mangeshkarji. On my request, Lataji sent me a few recordings of her father. It was Dinanathji's aesthetics and approach that inspired me to create Mangresh. This raga has the same notes that I had heard Dinanathji use in his singing. Lataji suggested the name Mangresh to me.

Kamalshree (1991)   *Evening raga*

I was shocked when I heard of Rajiv Gandhi's assassination. He was very fond of music and I remember his presence at some very memorable concerts. This raga is a beautiful blend of Raga Shree and Raga Kedar.

Ganesh Kalyan (1992)   *Evening raga*

I presented this raga at the historic Ganesh Festival that takes place every year in Pune. I was inspired greatly by the elephant god and played this raga as a prayer and offering to Lord Ganesha. Raga Shudha Kalyan, Yaman Kalyan and Raga Jaijaiwanti are the inspirations of this raga.

Subhalakshmi (1992)   *Evening raga*

This raga is a tribute to my wife, Subhalakshmi, who sacrificed her dance career for the family. It is also a tribute to all those great women who have sacrificed their lives for their families. It is my dream that one day every child is known even by his/her mother's name. This raga was inspired by Raga Shiv Ranjani, Raga Patdeep and the Kannada family of ragas.

Rahat Kauns (1997)   *Night raga*

I performed this raga for the first time in Mumbai in 1997. It is my humble tribute to my mother Rahat Jehan Khan. My mother holds a very special place in my life and whatever I am today, is because of her blessings. This raga was inspired by Raga Chandra Kauns, Raga Malkauns and the Kannada family of ragas.

Haafiz Kauns (1997)   *Night raga*

I had to offer a musical tribute to the memory of my guru and my father. With the blessings of my late father, Ustad Haafiz Ali Khan Saheb, I was able to create Raga Haafiz Kauns that conjured up a picture of him in my mind. This raga was inspired by Raga Rageshwari, Raga Malkauns and Raga Joge.